MEETING THE GLOBAL CHALLENGE

MEETING THE GLOBAL CHALLENGE

Establishing a Successful
European Industrial Policy

Martin Bangemann

*With a Foreword by
Sir Leon Brittan*

KOGAN
PAGE

Kogan Page is the UK member of the Euro Business Publishing Network.
The European members are: Les Editions d'Organisation, France; Verlag Moderne Industrie, Germany; Liber, Sweden; Franco Angeli, Italy; and Deusto, Spain. The Network has been established in response to the growing demand for international business information and to make the work of Network authors available in other European languages.

First published in Germany in 1992
by Verlag Bonn Aktuell GmbH

Published in Great Britain in 1992
by Kogan Page Ltd
Reprinted 1993.

Apart from any fair dealing for the purposes of research or private study, or criticism or review, as permitted under the Copyright, Designs and Patents Act, 1988, this publication may only be reproduced, stored or transmitted, in any form or by any means, with the prior permission in writing of the publishers, or in the case of reprographic reproduction in accordance with the terms of licences issued by the Copyright Licensing Agency. Enquiries concerning reproduction outside those terms should be sent to the publishers at the undermentioned address:

Kogan Page Limited
120 Pentonville Road
London N1 9JN

© Verlag Bonn Aktuell GmbH, 1992

British Library Cataloguing in Publication Data

A CIP record for this book is available from the British Library.

ISBN 0 7494 0858 8

Printed in Great Britain by
Ipswich Book Co. Ltd., Ipswich, Suffolk

Contents

Preface 7

Foreword 11

PART I
AN APPEAL FOR A EUROPEAN INDUSTRIAL POLICY 13

1 The Pros and Cons of Industrial Policy 15

2 Competition and Industrial Policy are not Opposites 24

3 The Best Example of Industrial Policy: The Single Market 36

4 The Strengths and Weaknesses of European Industry 52

5 The Industrial Policy Stimulus of Open Borders 66

PART II
IDEAS FOR EUROPEAN INDUSTRIAL POLICY: FIVE EXAMPLES   79

6 Quotas as a Sign of Weakness: The Motor Industry   82

7 Bundling European Interests: The Shipbuilding Industry   97

8 More European Cooperation: The Aviation Industry   106

9 The Key to the Future: The Electronics Industry   120

10 Creating a Consensus: The Biotechnology and Pharmaceutical Industry   135

PART III
BROADENING THE EUROPEAN DIALOGUE   149

Preface

This book has resulted from everyday political life. I see politics primarily as a joint search for solutions, even if the willingness to compromise is often considered a sign of weakness and a lack of principles. But without the willingness to talk between systems, the Cold War would not have been overcome and the ideals of European unity would have irrevocably been bogged down in the mire of national egoism from which it has had to free itself time and time again. He who is not willing to talk relies on superiority and not on arguments. What is accepted as unavoidable in politics, because politics is considered a dirty business anyway, generates fundamental objections, however, in economic policies. Talks between governments and industry are considered 'sins against free trade', especially in Germany and Anglo-Saxon countries.

Rumours and worse soon arise when politicians and businessmen meet. Thus, it is no surprise that so few managers move into politics or that very few politicians are willing to accept positions in industry. A switch from one side to the other is questionable and raises doubts about a person's independence and integrity. Politicians and business representatives carefully avoid each other. Industry does not comment on politics, and politicians carefully keep industry at an arm's length to avoid suspicions or malicious innuendoes. Consequently, neither side realizes its full potential. Both depend upon each other more than free trade purists or leftist critics of capitalism are willing to admit. We seriously need to discard ideology and relax the relationship between industry and politics. That is the purpose of this book.

Close contacts between politicians and industry are sometimes tolerated; for instance, the initiation of an education programme or a fresh impetus given to the economy in eastern Germany. However, if a minister for economic affairs tries to procure foreign orders for 'his' industry, he is attacked from all sides – something that happened to me during my time as the German Federal Minister for Economic Affairs. Consequently, pro-industry politics are usually conducted discreetly. It is only rarely that they are conducted boldly and in the open. I consider this to be a big mistake: industry needs political support as much as politicians need a strong economic basis to achieve political goals. I, therefore, support an open and relaxed relationship between industry and politicians – a relationship which is discussed openly and which allows definition of clear-cut social priorities. I do not understand 'industrial policy' to mean accommodating industry. Quite the opposite. It would not help industry if politicians too readily fulfilled their every wish. But, then again, the limits of industry's endurance cannot be tested with impunity either.

European industry faces great challenges in the near future – challenges which it cannot overcome by itself. The European single market will remove national import barriers. We also have to further open our markets to eastern Europe. The European textile industry faces difficult times, as do car and electronics manufacturers. The sharp wind of competition is blowing into Europe from all sides, and it will not be easy to resist the temptations of protectionism if European industry is not prepared for this rough, worldwide competition now. In a situation like this, it is not sufficient to be pro-free trade. European industry must remain an important player, not only in the single market, but also in the world market. It must be the main goal of a European industrial policy to make sure this occurs.

The public discussion on industrial policy is still too strongly influenced by the old ideological dichotomy of free trade and planning. This overlooks the fact that generating international competitiveness under current world market conditions is a dynamic process in which governments also play an important role. Competitiveness cannot be bestowed upon an industry, it must be earned like everything in life. Operative competition is only one side of a market economy. The other is efficient social institutions, which alleviate structural changes. One such institution, which plays an important role in maintaining the competitiveness of European industry, is the Commission of the European Communities. This book describes how industrial policy is understood and conducted in Brussels. It will not contain any slogans or 'easy' solutions. Industrial policy is not for big simplifiers; it is the result of hard struggles for rational compromises. Purists of all persuasions will dislike it. I, therefore, dedicate this book especially to them.

Martin Bangemann
Brussels, January 1992

Foreword
by Sir Leon Brittan

This is a thought-provoking book. Martin Bangemann offers an extremely convincing analysis of what was so wrong about some traditional national concepts of industrial policy which involved, for example, locking favoured companies in a 'golden cage of subsidies', or offering protection from outside competition, and promoting champions. He makes a powerful case for the strictly horizontal application of national and Community policy, without sectoral bias. And he rightly lays stress on the primary duty of bureaucrats and of politicians to set a clear regulatory framework rather than to second-guess the market within that framework.

It is almost axiomatic, however, that if a book is to say anything interesting, it should provoke dispute as well as agreement. Few readers, I suspect, will accept everything in this book. There is much, indeed, that I would dispute myself, particularly about the limits of competition policy and the extent of market intervention which may be desirable in particular cases. But that only illustrates why the subject matter is so relevant and so interesting. This book is an important contribution to a debate which is central to Europe's future.

Part I

AN APPEAL FOR A EUROPEAN INDUSTRIAL POLICY

Industrial policy is a dazzling term which everybody uses differently. Even the most direct interpretation, a 'policy for industry', does not quite fit, for what is beneficial for industry? It is quite often the opposite of what industrial associations demand from politicians. Which association wants more competition or more stringent environmental standards? Both, however, are in the best interests of industry, even if the short-sighted say differently. Demanding a European industrial policy is even more likely to cause trouble, as the term 'industrial policy' is understood to mean various, even opposite, things in the European Community. This circumstance makes it especially necessary to define the term 'European industrial policy'.

I understand 'industrial policy' to mean creating international competitiveness. There is no simple method to do this. Competition is just as necessary as governmental support for any structural changes to occur. Research, education, transportation and communication networks are, however, equally decisive factors for competition. Industrial policies must be open to discussion. Only those solutions which rectify competitive weaknesses and improve strengths are important. This 'horizontal approach' to industrial policy does not try to help selected sectors, it attempts to improve competitiveness from the bottom up and is increasingly gaining support in the European Community. I cannot say there have not been occasional setbacks, however. This new application of the term industrial policy is not to be dogmatic. I think that it deserves a more extensive explanation and will give one in the first section of this book. Each of the following five chapters will illuminate a different aspect of European industrial policy.

1

The Pros and Cons of Industrial Policy

There are few economic topics in the European Community which are discussed as emotionally and controversially as the pros and cons of industrial policy. This was the case when I was Federal Minister of Economic Affairs in Bonn. Shortly after I assumed that office, I announced, perhaps unwisely, that I was not an orthodox market economist. By making this statement, I gained the reputation of being unreliable in economic policy – the worst reputation a German minister of economic affairs can be accused of having. In the Federal Republic of Germany, industrial policy is still a strict taboo, although domestic coal, the Airbus and the *Bundesbahn* (railway) are subsidized with billions of marks. As strange as this may seem, it is not seen as a contradiction to the economic ideology Germans tend to preach around Europe. Our partners naturally notice the contradiction between ideals and reality and are, accordingly, sensitive or irritated when Germans begin to moralize.

The German reunification has necessitated the use of unorthodox methods. As a result, economic moralizing has lessened, but a deeprooted German distrust of everything called industrial policy remains. These misgivings are not completely unjustified, as industrial policy often hides the economic belief that market planners are more reliable than forces of a free market. Nevertheless, I still use the term industrial policy for two reasons: first, because it does not have these negative connotations everywhere in the European Community (indeed, in some regions people attach high hopes to it); and second, because I firmly believe that an economic industrial policy, which combines a free market with the courage to make political decisions, is possible. This type of industrial policy, especially, needs explaining as it confirms neither the fears of the one side nor the hopes of the other.

RECOGNIZING THE GOVERNMENT'S RESPONSIBILITY

Before anything else is said, the worst possible type of industrial policy is that which is conducted half-heartedly and with a bad conscience. It will only waste money because its economic goals are not well defined and, consequently, are not open to discussion. When well-defined economic principles are lacking, those complaining the loudest are often the ones who receive the most money. This is the way industrial policy is conducted in those countries which, at least officially, condemn it the most. Consequently, industrial policy is defined solely by industrial goals and not by public interest. Surely, it would have been more appropriate to have had an industrial policy which would have developed a modern train system and invested in new, high-speed railways, for example, instead of being satisfied with only balancing the losses of the German *Bundesbahn* over the years. The ICE will probably arrive ten years late and the magnetic train system will possibly never be integrated into the public transportation network. These are, unfortunately, the bad results of a half-hearted industrial policy.

The ideological fight in the European Community concerning industrial policy has long obscured the role governments necessarily play in modern economies – the role of a catalyst and pathfinder for industry. Government orders exceed 50 per cent of total orders in some branches of industry and are, as a result, important factors in such decisions as whether copper wires or ISDN networks will be installed, whether plain typewriters or integrated office systems are placed in offices, or which type of telephones are installed by the telephone company. The manner in which government contracts are awarded, whether simply accepting current technical standard or demanding innovative solutions, is also an industrial policy, whether critics are willing to admit it or not. A government which buys products an industry wants to sell and not what it actually needs should not be surprised if its 'royal purveyor' no longer goes to the trouble of developing products which would be competitive on the world market. Supply is always only as good as demand.

This is not to say that governments should be able to recognize future markets better than businessmen. It would be a great accomplishment, however, if governments, as customers, were to use their enormous buying power to become more efficient and effective in conducting their own affairs. All too often it is industry which forces its obsolete technical standards upon governments, instead of governments defining public goals which must be met by industry. Most public buyers avoid risks and select the cheapest offers, afraid of making wrong decisions, which could be uncovered and publicized by auditors. In terms of industrial policy, however, this is a questionable strategy as it forfeits the enormous opportunity of technical innovations.

The least intelligent way of conducting industrial policy is buying or subsidizing the obsolete technologies of domestic industry. A negative example is the European telecommunications industry. For a long time it profited from government orders but, at the same time, lost ground on international markets. Supporting domestic industries by locking them in a golden cage of subsidies has never been successful. This is no great surprise as governments do not know a future winner any more than the companies do themselves. It is unlikely that a civil servant will be better at forecasting markets than highly specialized managers and businessmen. The only reason governments are asked to help define 'future industries' so often is that, in doing so, they are also obliged to help carry the financial burden of any wrong decisions. Whatever is studied, tested and produced in cooperation with the government, and paid for by public funds, receives a seal of approval which almost automatically guarantees the privilege of continuous subsidies should the project fail. In this manner, hopeful projects quickly become hopeless subsidy cases.

... BUT REJECTING GOVERNMENT PRESTIGE OBJECTS AND PROTECTIONISM

The list of government-subsidized 'investment ruins' is roughly the same length in every country of the European Community. Practically every government failed to resist the temptation of developing future technology with government funds or of saving established companies from ruin. Only rarely has such a policy been successful, for example the French TGV or the Airbus. Usually, attempts to uncover future markets or to revitalize past successes fail miserably. Subsidizing government prestige objects has little to do with a future-oriented industrial policy, as it is based on a misconception of industrial policy. This mistake already occurs with the financing of a few 'demonstration projects' or balancing money-losing undertakings. There are always good reasons to do this, but it will hardly help recover a nation's international competitiveness.

Subsidies are financed by those companies and medium-sized firms which are currently competitive and which do not receive government funds. Large subsidies lead to high taxation, weakening the competitiveness of exactly those companies which are the basis of a healthy economy. A sectional industrial policy, ie a policy which is oriented on the interests of a single branch of industry, soon depletes a country's financial resources and weakens its own productive basis. Quite often, the political courage is lacking to correct mistakes and withdraw from subsidized projects. The subsidy spiral accelerates. One evil soon attracts another: first, governments fund research; next, production losses are balanced; finally, punitive tariffs are placed on foreign competitors who, in spite of domestic subsidies, still have lower prices. This is the industrial policy nightmare of replacing entrepreneurial responsibility with government planning.

The final resort of a subsidizing industrial policy is protectionism. It is seldom difficult to find parliamentary majorities for such measures. Protectionism is easily rationalized with demagogic means. Patriotism is appealed to. Foreign rivals are slurred. The reasoning is always the same: why do we need foreign cars, steel, or coal? Do we not produce high quality cars, high-grade steel, or energy ourselves? Such a view is often more popular than one which advocates free trade. No one is willing to fight for consumer interests but many are willing to fight for endangered jobs, although the workers, as consumers, do not necessarily buy domestic products.

Free trade does not have many friends when the going gets rough. The latent fear of foreign products is most easily allayed by direct investments by foreigners. Even dyed-in-the-wool protectionists are suddenly converted when foreign car manufacturers create safe jobs in the politicians' own constituencies. Direct investments are the best way to protect free trade on the political level as well. Without faith in open borders, there can be no final willingness to change. People basically like to leave things the way they are. Economic lethargy, however, leads directly to a loss of economic competitiveness and jobs.

Rational industrial policies should not circumvent competition. Quite the opposite, industrial policies should nourish and defend competition. The European Community needs a lot of this type of industrial policy. The realization of the single market offers the unique opportunity to start anew. The numerous national import barriers, for example, for third-country cars, toys or porcelain, will have to make place for the liberal dynamics of the single market. Strict national import barriers require border controls, not only at the borders of the producing countries but also at the borders of partner countries to avoid imports circumventing national border controls. Unless protective measures are enforced at all external borders of the Community, individual national protectionism will lose its basis in the single market as soon as border checks are no longer conducted at the internal borders. There is, however, currently neither a majority in the European Council for such measures, nor would the Commission, which has the sole right to make such proposals, support them. This is the end for protectionist industrial policies which want to close borders. While it is not possible to say that there will never be transgressions on a European scale, the single market will be much more open than the twelve separate European markets are now.

One thing will definitely not occur, at least not with the current Commission: a repetition of subsidizing industrial policies which have already failed in the individual countries. Such failures occurred due to a lack of money or borders which were unable to repel foreign competition. This, however, is exactly what some people in the European Community have secretly hoped for: that measures which had failed nationally would somehow work on a European level. That import barriers would be set up by the European Community and replace national import barriers and, perhaps, that strategic industries could be subsidized by the Community as well. Subsidies which would, miraculously, make 'European champions' of the small 'national champions', supposedly enabling them to compete more efficiently with their strong Japanese and American rivals. Such was the daydream many politicians and industrialists dreamt. Luckily, this manner of protectionism did not succeed in becoming industrial policy. However, it failed not necessarily because its supporters were converted to free trade, but because common sense shows that it is simply impossible to isolate Europe from the rest of the world.

THE NEW MODEL OF INDUSTRIAL POLICY FOR THE EUROPEAN COMMUNITY

The change of attitude towards open competition was mainly achieved by a strategy paper on industrial policy which, following my recommendation, was adopted by the Commission in the autumn of 1990. The paper stated clearly and for the first time that existing import barriers would not be replaced by Community quotas and must be removed by the end of 1992. Furthermore, it said that the old, sectoral industrial policy would be replaced by a modern, horizontal approach which would no longer support individual industrial sections but competitiveness on a large scale. Few had expected such economic courage from the Commission and, correspondingly, the response was extremely positive.

Was this the final victory of free traders over protectionists? I doubt it. Caution is required, if only for the reason that political victories are never final. Victories are only decisions which can already be revised on the next day. The economic principles defined in that paper on industrial policy will have to survive everyday life. Principles count very little when a hundred thousand jobs are endangered. Free trade policies have to prove time and time again that they provide better results than subsidizing industrial policies. These policies are still very much alive in many heads. Many firm believers in free trade lose this trial of nerves. This can be seen from the lack of results in eliminating subsidies and in encouraging deregulation in the Community.

There are other reasons for caution: not only protectionists must learn from past mistakes. Dogmatic free traders must also realize that in modern economics it is not sufficient solely to define clear and predictable goals for an economy. Nevertheless, this by itself is an enormous feat of economic learning for most and one which is not yet finished in all of the member states. Decisive, competitive advantages are not permanent, they have to be regained each day. It is not sufficient to only protect competition. Ever more often, it is necessary to first create competition before it can survive on its own. Competition policies are primarily passive: they remove barriers to competition. In comparison, industrial policies are active: they create competition. Competition requires two (or better, more) competitors. Defending free trade can only prevent fusions and not produce strong competitors who are able to survive in international markets. This is something only industrial policies can do. For this reason, it is fundamentally wrong to place economic policies in opposition to industrial policies.

A subsidizing industrial policy is doomed to fail. Not so a competitive industrial policy which is world-market oriented. The single market will be the perfect training ground for learning global competition. First, it will accelerate structural changes in the European Community, which, again, will create further changes.

Second, the single market is synonymous with deregulation and liberalization. My predecessor as Commissioner and the intellectual father of the single market, Lord Cockfield, once said that if all had known how much more competition the single market would result in, the European industry and, surely, the European governments would have been against it. Back then, the single market was the last chance for the sclerotic, paralyzed European economies. These economies, totally unable to make the tremendous reforms which were required, were slowly but surely losing ground to their American and Japanese competitors. This desolate outlook forced them to accept the principle of majority decisions without which the single market would have never been completed. Now, governments must advertise for bids in the whole Community and products can be marketed without changes on all European Community markets. Competition will increase at all levels, from suppliers, to manufacturers, to sales.

In future it will be possible to supply and maintain this huge single market from a single site. It will no longer be necessary to maintain branches in several of the member states to circumvent import barriers. It is a new beginning. Investors from non-European countries can start anew in 1992. They can construct production facilities at a new location and start with a relatively young and adaptable team. European companies, however, are more tightly bound to their old and often less advantageous production sites. The removal of national import barriers will relentlessly uncover competitive weaknesses of currently protected industries. This may not distress orthodox economists who are of the opinion that industries which are no longer competitive will simply have to close down. This standpoint may be true in theory, but we will never achieve our goal of a huge single market if we 'live and let die'. National protectionist measures are still in existence and governments will only remove them if they are no longer needed, ie if an industrial policy makes them obsolete. To expect anything else would be foolish.

THE THREE MAIN QUESTIONS OF EUROPEAN INDUSTRIAL POLICY

An industrial policy must accept things as they are and not as policy makers might wish them to be. There are three basic questions which must be answered. First, is an industrial policy really needed or can the market take care of itself? Second, if for whatever reason government action is required, what should its goal be? Finally, in what way, in what time, and by which means is this goal to be achieved? The first question concerning the necessity of industrial policy is already controversial by itself. No one doubts that European semi-conductor manufacturers have significantly lost ground on the international market. But what should the consequences be? Is it true that no single country can be the leader in all fields and that there are enough semi-conductors as there are? Or, is it true that a technological dependence upon non-European semi-conductors would impair other European industries, that the Community cannot simply surrender this golden key to its future? There is no single answer to be found to this seemingly simple question, neither in industry nor in politics. Questions such as these can only be answered in close collaboration with the corresponding industry and its customers.

For this reason, politicians and industrial representatives must not avoid each other. Both have separate responsibilities which may not be confused. Industry is primarily responsible for itself. However, can one let the medium-sized companies of the machinery industry suffer because European semi-conductor manufacturers have lost contact with the top of the market? Can one simply let the customers of these manufacturers be forced to hand over their precious software know-how to Japanese competitors in order to obtain these indispensable semi-conductors? Such questions cannot be answered with a simple 'yes' or 'no'. It is only rarely possible to answer questions of industrial policy in this manner. If industrial policy action is required for semi-conductors, what should be done? Is technological independence required or is it sufficient that European companies have the basic know-how? What follow-up action is needed for which goals? There are questions upon questions and only rarely are there simple answers. Industrial policies cannot be completely consistent. There is no book of rules for industrial policy action. Politicians cannot refuse to be involved, however, as they will, sooner or later, be forced to act when difficult situations do not quickly improve by themselves.

WHAT IS THE ALTERNATIVE?

Politicians may not ignore reality. The question which cannot be repeated often enough is: What is the alternative? The lack of a visible industrial policy results in a concealed industrial policy, disguised as a social, research or regional policy. Competition policies can be used in such a manner that they become anti-competitive, ie, when certain structures are kept as they are.

Democratic societies do not sit still when whole industrial sectors or regions perish. Consequently, politicians are not always able to select the questions they would like to answer. This is something only science is able to do, to look for clear-cut answers under simulated conditions. Society, however, is not a testing field for scientific hypotheses. If industrial policy cannot find answers to important questions of everyday life, somebody else will, and their answers will certainly be less pro-free trade than my type of industrial policy.

It is easy to criticize an industrial policy. It is, however, much more difficult to find realistic alternatives. One instructive example is the opening of the single market for non-European cars. I support the opening of the single market for cars. Nevertheless, to achieve this goal we need the assistance of those countries whose car markets are currently protected by import barriers. I did not create these barriers; they exist and cannot simply be ignored. The aim of a single market is only achievable if the restrictive countries participate as well. This again requires that these countries are given time to restructure their car industries. Such intermediate solutions are hard to accept for free trade purists. The alternative, however, is a status quo which no one wants either.

Protectionists must be persuaded to cease their subsidizing industrial policy, and orthodox economists have to admit that ideal societies do not exist. A European industrial policy must find a reasonable compromise between these two extremes – a position which is the most difficult of all to defend. As little as subsidies are apt to disappear by themselves, can industrial policy be conducted against the market? I recommend a pragmatic industrial policy and, as such, I am truly not an orthodox free trader. An economy is not a closed system in which politicians are only spectators. This is especially true for a European industrial policy which must face its responsibilities. Industrial policy must be conducted purposely and not simply be a result of political coincidences.

2

Competition and Industrial Policy are not Opposites

The main goal of European industrial policy is increasing international competitiveness. On the single market and especially on the world market, European companies compete with other companies which operate worldwide and which maintain manufacturing facilities in several countries. Increasingly, the world market decides the fate of an industrial strategy. The time is gone when companies could quietly set up business in their own country without being disturbed by foreign competition. They were also frequently supported and subsidized by their government. Now, the direction and speed of economic developments are mainly determined by the world market. It is much easier to overcome protective, national barriers from outside than for a subsidized company to venture forth from within these barriers and conquer the world market. For this reason, manufacturing and, increasingly, service industries must be globally oriented. Nationally-oriented production deliberately ignores the world market without being able to keep international competitors out of its domestic market. Every profitable market will be discovered and supplied, sooner or later, by a globally operating company. No government can deny its citizens and industries the ability to buy products of their own choice for an extended period of time. Consequently, government protection is increasingly losing its appeal.

EUROPEAN INDUSTRY MUST FACE THE WORLD MARKET

Import quotas are the worst way to admit one's own weakness. There is no form of advertisement which is less positive. Import quotas also damage the domestic economy, as cheap imports not only compete with domestic products but are also raw materials for other domestic industries which compete internationally. It is no longer possible for an economy to ignore international division of labour. Protection for one sector means higher costs for another. Accordingly, import barriers or high import levies damage an economy more than they help it. Protectionist measures always result in counter-measures which would especially hurt the exporting industries of Europe. Superior products always find a way to their customers, if not by imports then by direct investment in the protected markets. There is no alternative: European industry must face global competition if Europe is not only to be an important market but to stay an attractive production site as well. There are two industrial policy consequences: national import barriers, relics of an earlier protectionist era, must be abolished and European industry must be strengthened in order to be able to compete worldwide. As such, a European industrial policy strengthens competition and competitiveness.

The products of European industry must be present in all markets of the world. German industry, especially, with its annual export total, shows how to produce successfully for the world market. In the long run, it is not sufficient to be the world champion in exporting. Global orientation increasingly requires an on-site presence in the most important world markets with one's own production and research facilities. The large dollar fluctuations in recent years have shown all Germans how important it is to produce on-site. For many companies without production facilities in the US, the low exchange rate of the dollar led to large losses in the American market. Several companies now regret that they do not or no longer have American manufacturing facilities.

... AND BECOME A 'GLOBAL PLAYER'

European car manufacturers, in particular, are still too oriented on domestic markets. VW, Renault, and Fiat are strong in Europe but are far from being able to compete with the Japanese as 'global players'. In the long run, this could become a serious competitive disadvantage. In comparison, the chemical industry is traditionally present in the world market. It not only creates production facilities in third countries but also invests heavily in worldwide research – something which facilitates access to top international research. A global network of research and development centres makes it easier to close research deficiencies and to utilize the specialized know-how of other countries. A majority of the patents in biotechnology or ecological technology held by European chemical companies were not developed in Europe but in the foreign, mainly American, research centres of these companies. This is the result of global orientation which could be a role model for other industries. However, it should not result in a loss of technological competence in Europe. Quite frequently production facilities are placed where research is conducted. As long as a global strategy is purposely conducted, it is positive. If, for instance, it is conducted more half-heartedly, as in biotechnology, it requires industrial policy counter-measures to avoid the loss of jobs.

The first to conduct global business strategies were American companies: Coca-Cola, American Express and McDonald's. They became the original 'multinationals'. In recent years, Japanese companies have increasingly become real multinationals; at an almost breathtaking pace they have become present in all important markets of the world. Europe has become a favourite goal, not least due to the fear of European barriers. This fear lacks a basis but has still attracted several foreign investors. It is one of the few cases where incorrect rumours have had a positive result. On the other hand, European companies have still not discovered Japan even though similar rumours exist about it. The minimal presence in the Japanese market of European companies that have their own research and production facilities in Japan is difficult to overlook. However, it is even more difficult to draw reasonable conclusions for an industrial policy from these facts.

Currently, many European managers look primarily at middle and eastern Europe. Helping our eastern neighbours is one side of the coin; the other side is that, in the long run, our industries expect an economic advantage from this help. Sentimentality is misplaced. Reality will, sooner or later, catch up with companies which are investing in middle and eastern Europe to avoid the strong competition of the world market. Eastern markets only seem to be easier; they should not only be seen as markets for selling. Investments in Poland and Hungary will only be profitable if the Common Market can be supplied from there. Short-term exportation of industrial goods will force its way back into our markets in the long term. Consequently, this will cause competition to increase also.

THE WORLD MARKET AS A NEW AND 'RELEVANT MARKET'

One fact should not be overlooked: our industries are competing in the world markets with Japanese and American companies which are mostly larger, have more financial reserves and are globally-oriented. However, size alone does not guarantee international competitiveness; it sometimes even hinders by making companies less flexible. Nevertheless, large companies have a definite advantage in the research, development and marketing of new products. A minimum size is required to build a global sales network and, even more so, to erect modern production facilities in all of the important markets of the power triad: Japan, the US, and Europe. However, this is necessary if we are to participate in the ever more expensive innovation contest. For example, it was not possible for the multinational company Sony to force its video recording system upon the world market. Philips, the largest European competitor, had even less of a chance to make its system the world standard, although the Philips system was considered technologically better. However, compliments do not sell a product. Only the first to arrive in a market makes a profit; being second can cost a lot of money. Technological half-lives, the time required for a product to become technologically obsolete, are becoming ever shorter. This raises the stakes for those wanting to play at the top.

A European competition policy must be completely aware of the global dimension of competition. Currently, the 'relevant market' used for competitive evaluation of company fusions is only rarely defined by national borders. It is usually the single market, if not the world market, in which companies compete. This is a direct result of the increasingly global orientation of markets. Companies are widening the radius of their sales and are less willing to limit themselves to their domestic or even regional markets. The increased dimension of markets has led to larger returns and less costs, a result of the European single market. When companies are able to make longer production runs, investments and increasing costs for research and development amortize faster. It is easy to see that an increased European or worldwide orientation of markets will allow an even larger manufacturing scale for many products. This technically-induced trend to longer production runs is amplified by the enormous costs for research and development, global sales networks and the tendency to buy brand names. All in all, it results in a global competition of large companies. However, the number of competitors is no indicator of the intensity of competition. For example, the world has only three manufacturers of large aircraft and because of this there is a battle over each order. Competition is hard and sometimes goes beyond what is lawful.

SIZE DOES NOT AUTOMATICALLY MEAN A MONOPOLY

Multinationals are mistrusted by everyone. A widespread prejudice says that these large companies have only one goal, ie, to become bigger and stronger. Instead of efficient production methods and high-quality goods, they are primarily interested in controlling markets and making monopoly profits. This creates an insurmountable incompatibility between competition policies and industrial policies: the former are good for small companies whereas the latter only help big companies – or, to be extreme, the one side is good, the other side is evil. Obviously, even economic policies need simplistic enemies and, if possible, personified enemies as well. It appears to be the only way to sell the dull subject, economics, to the masses. But size does not necessarily correspond to market power. When market barriers are low and newcomers can easily enter this profitable market, monopoly profits quickly shrink in size. As a result, each individual case of fusion between large companies should be checked as to whether it will reduce or perhaps increase competition by attracting new competitors.

It may be difficult to explain, but my type of industrial policy intends to increase and not reduce competition. There is no doubt that concentration processes must be watched closely, for occasionally they do require close observation. There are 'dinosaurs' whose current size is only a result of past economic performance or government support. Some try, usually unsuccessfully, to maintain their current position solely by taking over their competitors. But, all in all, criticism of the large companies is based on a major misconception of the relationship between industrial policy, the single market, company sizes and competitiveness. First of all, it is not the single market or industrial policy that leads to large companies. Rather, they are a result of the global interconnections between markets and of technological innovations which, in some markets, require companies of a certain size in order to survive global competition. This is the case, for example, for aircraft, cars, semi-conductors and chemical products. European companies are seldom the largest or rarely dominate their market. When compared on a basis of turnover or number of employees, Japanese or American companies are almost always significantly larger. This fact is usually ignored when equating size and market position. When measured on a global scale, many European giants shrink rapidly. Of the world's ten largest banks, none are European. The European single market is the best solution for global competition: a large domestic market is the best training ground for the world market.

A reasonable industrial policy must help European industry grow to a size which will be globally competitive. Growth should not be hindered unless intolerable monopolies result. Size itself is not deplorable. An industrial policy should take the requirements of international competition into consideration as well as the needs of a vigorous domestic market. This is only possible with a dynamic and not a static competition policy. A prerequisite is the realization that the single market enlarges the relevant market for the companies. Domestic markets often have only enough room for a single, dominant supplier or several small sub-optimal-sized companies which are hardly internationally competitive. In the first case, competition suffers and in the second, economic performance. The single market is a solution to this dilemma. It ensures that all companies of the Community which do business in the same sector are forced to compete with each other as the barriers have been removed. The resulting increased competition will create companies which will be large enough to compete internationally. The single market will increase and not decrease competition.

LARGE AND SMALL COMPANIES ARE SYMBIOTIC ... NOT OPPOSITES

Each company must determine its optimal size itself. Just as industrial policies should not be regarded as creators of companies, should competition policies be used to artificially preserve certain business sizes? It is much better to enable small- and medium-sized businesses to challenge large companies than to hinder company growth. An entrepreneurial culture must be generated in which companies of all types and sizes can survive: small, medium and large companies, high-tech, mid-tech and low-tech, and industrial businesses and services – businesses which will complement each other optimally. This is the real strength of an economy. Large- and medium-sized companies are only rarely direct competitors; far more often they complement each other. Whereas large companies specialize in mass production, small- and medium-sized companies tend to specialize in custom-made products. This is not necessarily less profitable than mass production. The medium-sized industry is even usually more adept at finding economical niches and offering tailor-made solutions than bigger companies. This is where small companies can play out their trump cards. In recent years, small- and medium-sized companies have been the mainstay of the economy and have created more jobs than the larger companies. The single market will help them. The fragmented domestic markets are often too small to make the manufacture of specialized products profitable. With the removal of national barriers, these small- and medium-sized companies will profit also. Border checks are only a bothersome expense for large companies; for small companies, however, they are a big deterrent.

A successful economy not only needs big 'flagships' sailing the seven seas but also small and agile 'schooners' which deliver, supply and ensure that the high quality products arrive in time. Many small- and medium-sized companies are suppliers for globally operating and competing companies. This is a type of symbiosis: both sides are equally bound to and dependent upon each other. It is not always easy to say which of the two depends more strongly on the other. An increasing number of large companies are realizing that their depth of production, ie, the amount of components which they produce themselves, is too large. They react by subcontracting individual production sectors or services, for instance advertising, construction departments or laboratories. Medium-sized companies are the main ones to profit from this subcontracting as they are able to adapt capacities more easily and often have special know-how. The result is a fertile division of labour between large-, medium- and small-sized firms in which each type of company concentrates on what it does best. Small is not always weak, and unprofitable and big is not always strong and powerful. These prejudices no longer have much to do with reality. The economy only has strong and weak companies. The assignment of companies to categories, ie, profitable and non-profitable, is determined by business strategies and not by business sizes. Anyway, the number of wrong decisions made by a company tends to increase with size.

This is the reason that I am not a friend of policies oriented on medium-sized companies – policies which automatically assume that small- and medium-sized companies need subsidies. Small companies do profit, albeit indirectly, from the market power of big companies and vice versa. The numerous small- and medium-sized suppliers and service businesses do profit if large companies with their financial strength and enormous technological potential are able to survive in the treacherous international markets. It would be completely wrong to pit large and small companies against each other: they are very much dependent upon each other. Competent surroundings are a prerequisite for competitiveness. This includes flexible and highly specialized suppliers who continually improve their products. However, medium-sized suppliers should not be dependent upon a single large company if they are to fulfil their innovative role. This is not in the best interests of large companies either, as only strong and self-confident medium-sized partners can compensate for the deficits which would otherwise make inert 'tankers' of these proud 'flagships'.

TESTING THE EUROPEAN COMMUNITY'S MERGER CONTROL

The ordinance regulating company mergers has brought about the necessary legal instrumentation to check, at a Community level, large mergers and takeovers of European importance. The selected checking procedure makes for fast reactions, enabling companies to create efficient business strategies. The decisive, legal criterion for competition is the 'relevant market', ie, the actual size of the market on which competition is conducted. This market will increasingly be the European single market. We will have to learn to think in larger dimensions. Nothing can be said against creating efficient economic units by merging, if competition in the relevant market is not impaired. The European merger control aims to do both: to enable companies to achieve an optimal size and to guarantee lively competition. These objectives do not contradict each other if one uses the right criteria for making the decisions.

The Commission, a board of 17 commissioners, has final jurisdiction on mergers of European dimensions. This is the object of occasional criticism that the method supposedly leads to questions of competition being decided on irrelevant data. It is in fact a good question whether the merits of mergers should be decided by the Commission or, better, by an antitrust agency. An independent agency first makes decisions based on competition issues. These decisions may then be reviewed by a higher-up, political unit which may take additional macro-economic facts into consideration. However, the practical difference to an independent antitrust agency is small. In a large majority of cases, the Commission follows the recommendations of the appropriate commissioner without a discussion. Difficult cases are decided politically anyway. German law requires that all aspects, including the industrial policy implications, of a merger be taken into careful consideration. I consider the Commission's single-step mode of decision-making to be better than the two-step German mode in which the antitrust agency passes the difficult cases to the Federal Minister for Economic Affairs for judgement. The German model leads to a much more politicized merger policy than the single-step Commission model as the final decision is more drawn-out.

The Commission decides behind closed doors and relatively quickly. In comparison, the German procedure is often prolonged as the Federal Minister for Economic Affairs is forced to decide about an exception to the regulations concerning mergers while standing in the limelight. Frequently, a sensible decision is no longer possible. Competition policy is often the loser in this public gauntlet running, especially when the antitrust agency actively participates in the political discussion, prejudging the petitioner. In this sense, the European merger control allows for much more objectivity, provided that all pertinent arguments are given the necessary consideration in advance. In the *Bundeskartellamt*, the German antitrust agency, aspects of competition are checked by experts in the corresponding field. In contrast, the responsible Commission services are isolated. It is imperative that the sector-related agencies are included in merger decisions as soon as possible in order to avoid political discussions resulting from different expert, I repeat, expert opinions on a merger. This is a technical shortcoming of the current mode of decision-making of the Commission. A shortcoming which must be eliminated in order to make more objective decisions.

The Commission is not a creator of European companies. However, the situation in which decisions are made is usually different from national situations. The ordinance is mostly applied to decide whether a border-crossing merger will impair competition in the single market. This is commonly assumed. Nevertheless, it is quite often less impairing than a national merger. As a result, it is not surprising that prohibitions of mergers are rare at the European level. This has nothing to do with anti-competitive industrial policies. It is a result of the larger relevant market. Horizontal mergers of domestic companies always lead to increased market shares and reduced competition. This is not necessarily the case when companies in different countries, whose markets did not previously overlap, merge. Competition may even increase as the new competitor can operate more widely, doing away with the final national barriers.

The single market must, increasingly, be seen as the relevant market when judging mergers. Current turnovers are not necessarily relevant. The single market is slowly coalescing. The legal framework exists but consumers and manufacturers will need a bit of time to react. It would be completely wrong to perpetuate current structures by judging border-crossing mergers by today's standards. This would definitely be a misuse of competition policy, and for industrial policy would mean a conservation of current structures. Industrial policies must not try to preserve old, non-competitive structures, but must pave the way for an internationally competitive industry in the European Community.

SUBSIDIES DISTORT COMPETITION

Classic industrial policy was definitely pro-subsidy. Government help is occasionally legitimate and well-founded, for example, in the case of regional policy to reduce the economic differences between rich and poor regions. European Community law only allows such subsidies in well-defined cases, as these subsidies distort competition. Subsidies support only those businesses receiving, and discriminate against those not receiving or not depending upon, government aid. In such cases, rules no longer apply equally to all. This is especially dangerous for industrial policy if the subsidies are used to create surplus capacities to the disadvantage of those companies who did not receive subsidies. Consequently, it must be determined for each subsidy whether the aim, for example, regional support or the saving of jobs, justifies the distortion of competition it will create.

This may or may not be the case. Industrial policy arguments must be taken into careful consideration when deciding on subsidies. Publicly-owned companies must be watched closely, as government tends to help them with generous capital increases or by covering losses. Previously, the distortion of competition by government aid was limited to the country of incorporation. In the single market, however, these state-owned companies are increasingly active as competitors in foreign countries. This is especially ticklish when recently privatized businesses are taken over by state-owned companies from other countries. Thus, it must be ascertained that government-owned enterprises do not utilize the rules of the market solely for their own good. The Commission is the referee in these cases, ensuring that everyone plays according to the rules of fair play. Government-owned enterprises must be allowed, however, to look for new partners or to merge with other companies. The question of ownership is irrelevant for merger control, but not so for subsidy control.

When deciding on subsidies, the main question is: what would a private investor do under similar conditions? If a government acts very much differently from a private investor, ignoring risk and profit, it must be assumed that a competition-distorting subsidy is being awarded – an action which may not be accepted. If publicly-owned enterprises participate in a market, they have to follow the rules. They may not receive unfair advantages of losses being balanced by the government or public investments in objects which again result in losses. In the past, governments were never very successful entrepreneurs. The Community's subsidy control will force governments to exercise even more restraint. It could possibly result in governments losing interest in these companies and privatizing them. Publicly-owned businesses have lost almost all importance for industrial policy anyway, as there is nothing they can do better than a privately-owned business.

Subsidies which are supposed to solve sectoral problems in single industrial branches must be viewed with a certain amount of suspicion. In the past, this was repeatedly used in the attempt to protect sectors from the effects of declining demand or increased international competition. Now, it is generally accepted that it is not possible to keep non-competitive industries artificially alive. However, the political courage is often lacking to act upon this knowledge. Market laws cannot be suspended by subsidies for long. The only justification for sectoral subsidies would be to allow industry enough time to adapt to new market conditions. Non-profitable capacities must either be reduced or modernized. Surplus production cannot ignore demand. This is the most expensive and detestable form of social policy: pointless work is almost worse than no work at all. Nevertheless, in terms of industrial policy, closing production facilities is not always the most rational solution. A shutdown should not be done without reason, as it is almost impossible to reactivate a closed facility: technicians leave for more profitable areas, lost know-how stays lost. Consequently, each case must be checked carefully as to whether there is a sound basis for a rescue operation or not. However, the industry itself must devise a convincing rescue plan early enough for a rescue to succeed. Sector-specific aid is only acceptable when accompanied by a convincing rescue plan.

SUBSIDIES ARE NOT ALL NECESSARILY EVIL

However, the duration of subsidies for individual industrial branches must be as brief as possible. If restructuring does not promise to be successful, then aid should focus on creating new jobs. In this case, it may be sensible for regional policy to concentrate on sectoral focuses purposely to create new jobs in depressed regions. It cannot simply be accepted that a whole region suffers because the main employer closes down. This calls for industrial policy to strengthen infrastructure, develop new educational centres and create new jobs. These horizontal measures which increase the attractiveness of a whole region are more preferable to measures which only balance individual losses. When employed to create new and competitive jobs and not to sustain doomed industries, subsidies can actually strengthen instead of weaken competition. Nevertheless, horizontally effective aids can warp competition and result in sectoral distortion, especially when used to support capital intensive investments which are expensive but only create few jobs.

Subsidies are *a priori* neither good nor bad. Although it is very necessary to reduce the number and amount of subsidies, aims and means must not be mistaken. Subsidies are a legitimate means of politics. However, they must be used to achieve a purpose. Consequently, the reduction of subsidies may not become a goal in itself. Political courage is required to set priorities. Weeding is as much a part of industrial policy as planting. Subsidies which are no longer needed or which have become damaging must be cut decisively; new political goals must be more clearly defined. An industrial policy which distributes a little bit to everyone will end up giving nothing. Sometimes it is necessary to increase subsidies slightly in order to decrease them in the long run. It is the goal that counts. Industrial policies need clear-cut decisions and not 'we'll get there somehow' measures. I prefer an industrial policy which lives up to its responsibilities instead of pleasant-sounding principles which cover up for sins. To sum up this chapter: competition and industrial policy are two sides of the same coin, and both equally important.

3

The Best Example of Industrial Policy: The Single Market

The single market is what domestic industries have been demanding for years: a domestic market of high purchasing power, unified technical standards and a lack of border controls which waste time and money. Following 1992, every product legally produced in the European Community may be marketed in all 12 member states at the same time. In the European Community national standards are either recognized or unified. European industry must no longer produce in line with various national standards and laws. This reduces production costs and increases the marketing range of products. The European consumer wins as well, having a larger range of products from which to buy and often at lower prices. The single market not only has the advantage of size but of increased competition as well. Initially, those interested solely in the larger market did not realize that competition would also increase. Now, however, even these last few have started their intensive preparations for 1992. The wailing of lobbyists and interest groups has lost its weight. There have been too many rapid changes for national governments to be easily interested in the egoistic goals of these groups. National slowdowns are increasingly less successful now that economic questions are decided in Brussels by a qualified majority.

THE SINGLE MARKET IS JUST THE BEGINNING

The single market is frequently just the beginning for further steps in deregulation and liberalization. Free trade forces national governments to review their own domestic regulations in order for their own countries to avoid losing appeal as business locations. One of the most regulated markets of the European Community is, for example, the pharmaceutical market. The price of medicine varies drastically due to the different social insurance systems within the Community. Prices are lower in countries where patients pay for a larger amount of their medicine themselves and higher in others. This will change when medicine is sold in the whole European Community. Wholesalers and retailers will buy where medicine is the cheapest. Health insurances will most probably not refund more than a medicine costs in another European country if this medicine can be imported with few problems. This will result in medicines produced in Germany being reimported via Greece or Portugal in order to benefit from the various profit ranges. Similar or identical medicines, or other products, will tend to have the same price in the whole Community. This will lead to substantial price reductions for medications in many EC countries. But this is not the end of it. The social insurance systems will be forced to adapt as well when the pharmaceutical industry starts pricing on an economic basis. One step of liberalization almost automatically leads to the next. These dynamics will make the single market the largest deregulation programme ever started in the European Community.

However, there is still a lot to do before the single market is completed. Although there have been no duty fees within the Community for a long time and the European Community's founding Treaty of Rome requires the abolition of non-tariff trade barriers, trade within the Community is still not pure free trade. When exporting goods to other countries of the Community, businesses must still, 30 years after the founding of the European Community, expect difficulties, albeit illegal difficulties, if their products do not fulfil national requirements exactly. The individual member states of the European Community have proven very innovative in creating new trade barriers. Foreign companies are currently only rarely discriminated against openly. EC law is now abided by, at least in this respect, in all countries of the Community. Nevertheless, governments try time and time again to give domestic industries unfair advantages by placing special demands on the production, marketing and labelling of products. The single market will alleviate this problem by the multilateral recognition or unification of these standards. This will allow traders and manufacturers to conduct transactions freely in the whole European Community. The resulting increased competition will be an advantage for the businesses themselves. Although they will no longer be able to hide behind national regulations, the competition in the single market will be a good preparation for the much harder competition in the world market.

The single market is exactly what European businesses need in order to practise for international markets. 'Go European' is the first step to global thinking. Businesses which succeed in the European single market have passed the acid test for the world market. Many European businesses would not have expanded beyond their cosy domestic markets if left to themselves. The single market is forcing them, sometimes quite brutally, to rethink. In the European Community, it is no longer possible to avoid confrontations with foreign competitors. This will get people used to new and different markets, resulting in increased willingness to conduct international activities. Several European companies have only just realized that they can supply (and could have supplied) foreign customers, despite significant difficulties, and that they can even create sales and production facilities in other countries. As such, the single market has given free tutoring to those companies which previously did not look beyond their domestic markets.

COMPETITION BETWEEN SYSTEMS AS AN IMPETUS FOR INDUSTRIAL POLICIES

It cannot be said often enough: the single market is the new, relevant market for European companies and will decide the success or failure of business transactions. This does not mean that the domestic basis has become unimportant. Quite the opposite: nowhere are customers more demanding than at home. The best example for this is German car production. German drivers are well known for being very demanding about rust protection and the paintwork of their cars. These demands are an advantage for the German car manufacturers. 'Made in Germany' stands for high quality and a long service life. This is primarily a result of demanding domestic customers. Creating competitive advantages always starts in one's own country. The performance of suppliers and the quality of the employees is closely linked to the local conditions of a facility. Globalization of business strategies cannot replace maintenance of the home base. Global competition is the expansion of domestic advantages by creating foreign sales facilities and moving certain functions to other countries to take advantage of lower wages, lower costs for materials or more favourable research conditions. It must not be forgotten when globalizing markets that decisive competitive advantages are the result of unique local conditions which must not be given up, even for the single market.

In terms of European industrial policy, this means that we cannot completely do without the incentive of national or even regional competition. Member countries and their regions must maintain enough freedom to develop an unambiguous image with which they can aggressively advertise, ie, low taxation or wages or by a special quality of work. For purposes of industrial policy, a levelling of location factors within the Community is totally undesirable. Even within a unified single market, incentives for differentiation and improvement are required. This is the real secret of the single market's success.

Many advantages of a location are linked to regional conditions which are based on traditions and centuries of experience. The strict, local concentration of successful industries is a good example. It is not a coincidence that flowers come from Holland, cars come from Germany and movies come from Hollywood. It is always a result of know-how acquired over a long period of time and special production and sales methods which cannot be easily copied. It is relatively easy to sell something for a reduced price – sooner or later, someone will come along who sells for less. Long-term competitive advantages must be based on more than just a price. Long-term success is based on competitive advantages which are part of a society and which enable an economy to make products and to develop production and sales methods faster than others, time and time again. This system-linked capability of innovation is itself linked to national location conditions.

RIVALRY STRENGTHENS COMPETITIVENESS

Strong domestic rivals are even more effective as an incentive for innovation than international competitors. With domestic competition, a lack of success cannot be excused with some mystifying explanation. Competitive chances are the same for both. Consequently, success or failure is a result of the company's own ability or inability. There are some elements of chance but they leave little room for excuses. Successful domestic rivals are, consequently, an even larger stimulus than international competitors. The domestic market is very prestigious and is something nobody likes to lose. Accordingly, it is fought over. BMW has indirectly had a great influence in the newly developed S-class series of Daimler-Benz. In the same way, Renault and Peugeot both won from their battle over French market shares for middle-class cars. Domestic rivalry must not be sacrificed to some mistaken megalomania in the single market. As important as large production series may be, rivalry between companies over the number one position in their home country is almost more important.

More so, as the proximity of a direct competitor makes demands for protectionism even less likely to be heard by one's government than in the case of a solitary domestic supplier. If number one competes successfully in the international market, it is rather difficult to believe number two when it laments over unfair dumping or trade transactions by foreign companies. If there were only a single European supplier for important sectors of the single market, internal competitive pressure would be reduced considerably. Consequently, size is not everything. The presence and strength of local competition is also an important factor in the development of competitive advantages. This is something which we cannot do without in the single market.

THE PRINCIPLE OF MUTUAL RECOGNITION SOLVES MANY PROBLEMS

The principle of mutual recognition within the European Community is a solution to the problem of increasing markets for enterprises without sacrificing the advantages of regional products and production methods. Differing technical standards concerning product safety, health, the environment and consumer regulations are frequently a basis for many types of trade barrier. For a long time the attempt to solve this problem was to unify regulations for individual products. The Commission has basically stopped this approach now. Harmonization of Community law has simply proven too slow and inefficient. Total technical harmonization has been replaced by the principle of mutual recognition. Every product which has been legally produced within one of the member countries can, principally, be sold within the entire European Community. Enforcing this principle is not as simple as it seems. Not everything is accepted just because it is sensible.

... BUT SOME PROBLEMS CAN ONLY BE SOLVED POLITICALLY

Academic circles consider systems competition to be the most unregulated realization of the single market. The reality is often slightly different. The member countries of the European Community are not always willing to let foreign products into their country without a fight. Reasons can always be found, especially in the food sector – one of the most difficult in the single market. Are French consumers being cheated if synthetic vinegar is sold in France as *vinaigre*? Can heat-treated yoghurt be sold as yoghurt? Is 'caviar ersatz' promising more than it can deliver? These daily issues regularly result in national import prohibitions and frequently lead to legal action against the respective country because of its breach of treaties.

We do not want to define a unified product quality. For example, every brewery can brew beer according to their own recipe; they can even advertise the method. The customer must know what type of beer he is drinking. Labelling, again, can lead to new trade conflicts. For example, the decision on the maximum alcohol concentration a beer may have and still be called 'free of alcohol' or even 'alcohol reduced'. The effort in these day-to-day decisions is largely ignored by the populace. The single market will just not work without any rules at all. The member countries are simply not willing to recognize every document and every label without an argument. Besides, these arguments are frequently based on fundamental differences in opinion on health and consumer protection. As a result, the countries continue to require that national regulations are met. The single market cannot survive without a minimum of unified regulations and controls to produce a certain amount of trust in foreign products. Critics who often hastily accuse us of centralism and pedantry should realize that it is the sectarian regulations of the individual countries that create these problems – problems which must then be resolved at Community level.

Such trade disputes are frequently only conducted about technical details. However, sometimes disputes are based on fundamental differences which must be solved jointly. Should the irradiation of foodstuffs be permitted or not? Which sweeteners, colouring agents, and preservatives should be permitted or forbidden? Should all pieces of furniture have low flammability? In licit cases such as these, we must either accept a segmentation of the market or define minimal requirements for technical and consumer safety for the whole Community. This is the only way to achieve a single market. There are over 100,000 different national regulations for food additives, most of which contradict each other. There is hardly one sweetener permitted for use in all member countries, and then only with differing maximum concentrations in the various products. A similar confusion exists concerning colouring agents and preservatives. We are far from a unified market for foodstuffs, or for almost any sector of special public interest.

The method used to destroy unity in the single market is almost always the same: a member state discovers a health or safety risk, for example in hazardous substances. This country releases a national directive, limiting or even forbidding production and use of this questionable substance. As long as there is no contradicting EC rule, the Commission usually accepts such a national solo. However, it cannot accept it if free trade is restricted in an excessive or discriminating manner or the Commission is already working on a harmonized regulation. A solo by one government usually encourages others to follow, albeit with slight differences and new and special exceptions to the rules. This subdivides the single market until the Commission can only suggest a harmonization which, at best, removes the trade barriers resulting from the different regulations, or, in the worst case, transfers the most restrictive solution to the whole Community, as done in the case of tobacco advertisement. The blessing and curse of Community harmonization are often close neighbours but they are always the result of an attempt to avoid something worse. This is sometimes highly frustrating.

THE SINGLE MARKET IMPROVES ENVIRONMENTAL PROTECTION

The European Unification Treaty, in which the goal of a single market is defined, requires the Commission to conduct harmonization at as high a level as possible. This is to prevent companies of one country from obtaining unfair competitive advantages over other countries with higher legal standards by using hazardous additives in food, by not using safety devices in machines or vehicles, or by circumventing environmental safety measures. Industrial policy requires common standards which are as high and as ambitious as possible, for only this will guarantee that European products can be sold all over the world. Environmental protection is proof of this thesis. It is extremely difficult to regain the lead in environmental protection. This is especially true in comparison with foreign competitors, who may procrastinate investing in environmental protection and thus achieve a competitive advantage. Such an advantage, however, is mostly deceptive and temporary. Sooner or later, these companies will be forced to invest in environmental protection as well. However, they will not have the experience and know-how of those pioneering companies. The need for environmental protection will create new markets. The fight against the greenhouse effect, against polluted water and the dying forests can only be won with great technological feats. Industry will only develop new measuring and control technologies, solar collectors or biotechnological methods for sewage treatment, if the government forces them, by law, or persuades them, by tax benefits, to do so.

... AND ENVIRONMENTAL PROTECTION CREATES NEW JOBS

The Overseas Economic Committee for Development (OECD) estimates the current global market for environmental products to be DM 130 to 180 billion annually of which DM 80 billion are spent in the European Community. This market is said to have extremely high growth rates. Ambitious environmental goals and high environmental standards will ensure that European suppliers of products for environmental protection will be forced to accomplish even greater technological feats. It will also ensure that they will be able to capture the lead in the global market. Lax laws would only let this chance escape unused, leaving this growing market open to others. High environmental standards are not damaging, at least not if they are defined responsibly and flexibly and do not demand the impossible. This again requires that industry and politics are fair to each other; something which frequently must still be learned. The need to distinguish oneself on the one hand and the tendency towards pretense on the other are, unfortunately, still widespread. However, slogans and 'green' sales tags do not constitute a responsible environmental policy. Decisiveness is the sole environmental effect of a policy – something many seem not to care much about.

If what the experts say is true, that the carbon dioxide emissions are responsible for the hole in the ozone layer, then the price for fossil fuels should actually be increased in order to reduce consumption. I would agree completely with this reasoning on industrial policy grounds even if it would result in large, additional costs for energy-intensive industries. It would be almost impossible to pass such consumption-related carbon dioxide taxation for political reasons because it would not burden nuclear energy as well. This would not fit into the simplistic picture that many have of environmental policy. The principle of causation cannot be divided indefinitely, as it would then lose its credibility and intrinsic persuasiveness. Sensible, just solutions in environmental policy cannot be found when beliefs start to replace facts.

CHEATING DOES NOT PAY OFF

I can still remember the 'battle of the catalytic converter'. A substantial portion of the blame belongs to industry because it fought far too long against introducing the catalytic converter. Initially rejected as technically impossible or too expensive, it suddenly belonged to the car's standard equipment. Industrial policy must ensure the predictability and credibility of the environmental policy. Nevertheless, the industry must stop dissembling to procrastinate stricter environmental standards. This trick only works once. Next time around, excuses are no longer credible and environmental politicians feel it necessary to go beyond what the industry admits to be barely technologically feasible.

Cheating does not pay off in environmental policy nor anywhere else. The environment will not profit from strict environmental standards in a few countries of the Community if, as a result, others lag even further behind. We must also ensure that environmental protection does not harm the goal of a single market. As mentioned earlier, environmental solos are becoming increasingly 'in vogue'. The best answer to this would be high and legally binding environmental standards for the whole Community. However, sometimes this can only be achieved with a certain delay. Consequently, such measures should be conducted gradually wherever possible. Two different norms should be defined: the first, a legally binding limit which is based on currently available technology and which can be met immediately by even the poorer countries; the second, a long-term target, should be based on the highest level which is currently defined by scientific and technological research. Tax benefits could be arranged for such measures. This guarantees a certain amount of environmental equality in the Community and creates a strong incentive for technological innovation. In this way, industrial and environmental policy can pull on the same side of the rope. Hazardous substances could be treated similarly: dangerous substances must be forbidden. If a substance is only suspected of being dangerous, general interdiction is hardly justifiable. It would, however, be possible to allow individual countries to pass stricter standards if a less hazardous substitute is available. The unity of the single market remains intact and health protection is not neglected. I will attempt to use this concept of Community adaptation for the first time for asbestos.

FAREWELL TO THE CONCEPT OF DETAILED HARMONIZATION

These examples have shown the enormous implications of the

single market on industrial policy. Depending on the strictness of consumer and health protection, different economic structures appear. In the past, technical standards were to be defined in detail by the legislative. Now, however, following the German example, industrial self-administration is called for. Only basic safety and health requirements which a product must meet to be legally eligible for sale will be defined by law. National standardization experts then decide which technical standards will fulfil the legal minimal requirements. The national experts consult with each other on a European level so that differing national standards do not – purposely or accidentally – result in trade barriers. The Commission is not interested in becoming a bureau of standards: it has neither the manpower nor the expertise for such a task. In any case, the regulations of the European Community could not be changed as rapidly as technology changes.

Legislative work has been greatly simplified by foregoing detailed technical regulations. The European Community must no longer establish the maximum decibel level for lawn mowers, for example, nor define the shape of a tractor seat that would qualify them for sale in the whole Community. This can be done by national standardization experts, reducing the work load of the Commission and freeing it from the false charge of wanting to control every last detail. This love of detail was only necessary because the individual members of the Community were so pedantic themselves that they would not allow a product in their markets which did not exactly fulfil their standards and sizes. The principle of mutual recognition is thus one of the most sensational achievements of the single market, as it shatters national arbitrariness and the standardization monopoly of individual organizations.

... AND WELCOME TO INCREASED SELF-ADMINISTRATION

Standards do not require legal definition if the industry can agree on them by themselves. Standards have always been a matter of private agreement and, as such, this new principle has a deregulating effect. Nevertheless, the efficiency of the European standardization procedure must be improved. Currently, almost 1,000 European technical standards have yet to be defined for the legal minimum requirements for the single market. Consequently, international standards should be used directly wherever possible. This will not only save time and effort, but also reduce difficulties with our trading partners. American and Japanese companies tend to assume that competition will make their technical standards the industrial standards and, as a result, show little interest in collaborating with international standardization bureaux. This, also, must change if the world is not to split into various trading blocs with differing technical standards.

This is not a danger in the European Community. Products made according to European standards are assured of meeting legal requirements whether produced in Germany, Spain, the US, or Korea. European industry could also do with a similar transparency of regulations concerning foreign markets. Before a refrigerator can be sold in Japan, for instance, the supplier must prove that it meets the special Japanese regulations in all details. Such a procedure can take years. This special proof of conformity is now only rarely required in the European Community. Normally the manufacturer's certificate which states that the product has been produced in accordance with EC regulations suffices. An official test certificate is not required. Even products manufactured according to a different standard are not barred from the single market. The manufacturers must only prove that their products take into account the concerns of public safety in the same manner as assumed in the European standards.

Our trading partners are not as generous. European suppliers would love to be able to say the same of the American and Japanese markets. The 'CE-stamp' – CE is the French abbreviation for European Community – which certifies conformity with EC laws for critical products, can even be used by any manufacturer in the world, and usually by self-certification only. Toys from Korea or China carry this stamp of approval as do toys from Germany or Great Britain. Nor shall this be changed in the future. However, the CE-stamp should not be mistaken to mean 'made in Europe'. The European Community needs a unique and unmistakable sign of European origin. The importance of European symbols for the single market is often underestimated. The frequent use of the European flag shows that manufacturers have now recognized the advertising value of such symbols. The flag is a proprietary symbol of the European Council; the European Community only borrows it. This makes it all the more important that European manufacturers have a symbol under which they can sell their products all over the world.

POSSESSION OF STANDARDS IS OFTEN POSSESSION OF THE MARKET

Limiting legal definitions to basic requirements does not mean that the goal of unified technical standards has been totally abandoned. We have only stopped attempting this by legal means: the industry will have to agree on common standards by itself. The majority of European standardization is already conducted in this unregulated manner, ie, without being forced to define the technical details of EC regulations. For example, standardization experts have discussed intensively the definition of the 'Europlug', a plug which should fit all European sockets. However, due to the differing installation regulations of the various countries, the attempt at harmonization was aborted. The only result of this effort is a pamphlet with the bland title 'Plugs and sockets: living with differences'. For reasons of industrial policy, the unification of technical standards is still very important. For many industrial sectors standardization is the key to European competitiveness. An old and true saying of standardization experts is: possession of standards is often possession of the market.

New technologies offer the unique chance to start with common European standards. However, this requires that standards are introduced immediately. If not, one company will create its own standards which can no longer be changed, and so capture a leading position in the market. The case of VCRs and PC software, for example, demonstrates how single suppliers can force their standards, which are not necessarily the best, onto a whole market. Quality for consumers stagnates and the competition is forced to pay high licence fees. This is an important field for the collaboration of European industrial policies. It is, however, primarily a responsibility of industry itself.

For the single market it is sufficient that all electrical devices which meet the basic technical requirements can be sold freely. It is nonsense, for industrial policy reasons, to produce a different type of plug for each segment of the European market. Changing this, however, is the responsibility of industry itself, which must agree on a European standard. The uneconomical suggestion that the consumer buys himself an adapter cannot be the solution. This is not the customer's idea of a single market. Nor does it help industry to be forced to produce 18 different plugs just for a place in the whole Community market. Not one of these plugs has a chance of international success. If Europeans cannot agree on a single plug, they can hardly expect others to be willing to accept it either.

THE SINGLE MARKET ALSO EXISTS FOR GOVERNMENT CONTRACTS

Another focus of the single market programme on which the

Commission has been working for a long time is the liberalization of the process of awarding government contracts. In the 1970s regulations were already drawn up that required requests for bids on government supply and construction contracts to be advertised in the whole Community. However, large sections, such as power and water utilities, transportation, telecommunications and public services, were exempt. Only about 4 per cent of government contracts in the European Community are currently awarded to foreign companies. If the private sector is included, about a fifth of all supply and construction contracts are imported. This reveals the amount of protectionism which still exists for government contracts in the European Community. It will not be easy to change as government contracts are almost always a matter of politics and frequently an election issue. Advertising the request for bids on government contracts in the whole Community would, in many cases, require a severe change in political structures which will only be hinted at here but not discussed.

Government construction and supply contracts are limited to a few industrial branches where, however, they often constitute more than half of the total demand. Governments or public enterprises buy 90 per cent of all locomotives, railway cars and telecommunication equipment. The relationship of these industries with the government is correspondingly close. The result is an extreme loyalty to these companies. Government demand is also important in space technology, computers and power stations. Governments have a very large direct and, via state-owned companies, indirect influence on which trains will be bought, which cellular telephone may be installed, or whether new nuclear power plants are built or not. The awarding of government contracts is pure industrial policy, even if nobody likes to call it that.

As of 1993, it will become mandatory to advertise for bids on government contracts in the whole Community, even for those areas which were previously exempt, for example, power and water utilities, transportation and telecommunications. It is suggested that public services should also be included. Public or semi-public contracts exceeding a certain value will have to be advertised in the whole Community. As with the restriction of government subsidies, this will possibly lead to a new surge in privatization of publicly-owned enterprises. Community-wide advertising of contracts will make it very difficult to follow egoistic, national goals. The Commission will keep a close eye on advertising to ensure that these laws are upheld. The laws improve the right of companies to a fair hearing and their ability to sue for damages. The improvements are the only way to ensure that government contracts are awarded according to law.

The mandatory opening of markets will completely change the situation for many companies which are very dependent upon government contracts. They will no longer receive a predetermined contract volume from 'their' government or municipal administrations but will have to compete with companies from all over Europe. They will be forced to look for innovations and lower production costs. As such, the free market will be finally forced upon those companies whose principal customer has been the government. On the other hand, it will no longer be possible to conduct politics by making the awarding of large contracts dependent upon conformity or using large contracts for regional job policies. This will have a profound impact upon the relationship between industry and government administrations.

EUROPEAN LAWS WILL ALSO BE REFORMED

Advertising for bids on government contracts in the whole European Community is also an important part of the single market. Businesses are beginning to adapt to these changes by forming multinational cooperations and creating branches in foreign countries. An increasing number of European companies no longer have a certain nationality but are, in the best sense of the word, multinational. Good examples are the American multinational companies in Europe, such as IBM, Ford, General Motors and Exxon. Several Swiss and Scandinavian companies are also developing an international character. These companies all own production facilities in several countries, including the European Community, and none of these facilities rules over the others. The employees are international from the top to the bottom level. Enterprises of this type, with Europe-wide networks of subsidiaries, research, development and sales facilities are increasing. Although national locations will not lose their importance, new types of European cooperation are developing for which the legal framework must be created.

Company law has not kept up with the Europeanization of companies. In cases of multinational mergers or subsidiaries, at least one partner is forced to conduct business under foreign company laws. This can also lead to tax disadvantages. Several European cooperations were never completed because the partners could not agree upon a common legal structure or on the location of the joint venture's headquarters. Companies wanting to do business throughout Europe should no longer be limited by national legal structures which result in uncoordinated taxation. A first step was taken in 1989 with the introduction of a European economic interest association. This has given bidder communities and non-commercial organizations a legal European status of their own. It is a beginning. The real breakthrough will come with the introduction of the independent legal structure: the European limited company, or Europe Ltd. This will supplement, and not replace, legal structures in national company laws. Europe Ltd, is only a suggestion. The future will decide whether this suggestion is accepted or not.

IS CO-DETERMINATION THE PROBLEM?

The goal is to enable companies from various member countries to merge or conduct joint ventures according to European law and not be hampered by national laws. I am positive that this simplification would greatly increase the willingness for such multinational cooperations. The ability to choose national or European law would lead to healthy competition between the various legal structures. Europe Ltd, would be forced to compete as well. Consequently, there is really no reason not to permit it.

Co-determination creates a problem for this type of legal structure. For some member countries co-determination is a 'sacred cow' and, for others, a provocation. Even the various trade unions in the European Community have two different minds about co-determination by law. As a result, the Commission did not even suggest unified co-determination. The various member states are able to choose between different models which are roughly equivalent in substance but differ in detail. I, personally, believe that co-determination is a very sound principle, not only for reasons of social policy but also of industrial policy. However, national characteristics must be taken into account and, therefore, the proposition is a sensible compromise.

My positive opinion of co-determination may come as a surprise to those who do not believe that co-determination and liberalism fit together. I am of the opinion, however, that only an economy which is based on a social understanding has the flexibility and adaptability necessary to survive the ever faster changes in economic structure. Communication, the subject of this book, must start in one's own company. The employees must be convinced of their own products, products which are going to be sold. Creativity cannot be compelled and, for this reason, I do not consider co-determination to be the competitive disadvantage it is occasionally said to be. I do not know of a single case where a large company left Germany because of co-determination.

SOCIAL DUMPING IS NOT A GOOD INDUSTRIAL POLICY

Occasional conflicts may be quite fertile and stimulating, but a successful economy needs a stable social basis, a basis which can only be created by the government, industry and its employees. There is a social side of the single market which must guarantee that basic social rights are given in the whole Community and which must prevent social dumping. High wages, ambitious environmental goals, or high-level social security are not competitive disadvantages, they are social goals which must be pursued aggressively. People must know what they are working for. Low wages, a polluted environment and social dependency will not inspire them to work. On the other hand, a society can only afford what it earns by competition. The social wealth of a society is primarily a result of its productivity. Therefore, the main goal of industrial policy must be the growth of productivity, thus creating the best conditions for sensible environmental and social policies.

It is not possible to unify social services dependent on productivity in the whole Community. It would remove the only competitive advantage of the poorer countries, their low costs, and financially overtax the more productive countries. The social gap between the individual countries of the Community must be closed by an increased economic growth in the poorer countries and not by an increased social transfer. This also means, however, that the wealthier countries cannot expect their higher social level to become the Community standard. He who wants to earn more but work less must be more productive. Each company will have to live with its own mistakes in the single market and these mistakes will be uncovered much more quickly due to international competition. This is the main reason for the economic dynamics which no member state can escape currently radiating from Europe. Not even the German shop closing law will remain unchanged in the single market. That, however, is not a reason to worry but a ray of hope. It shows that modern politics originate more and more in Brussels.

4

The Strengths and Weaknesses of European Industry

The classic theory of comparative advantages says that each country will specialize in the field in which it excels. International trade will ensure an economic benefit for all. This theory is still valid, but with a small but decisive difference. Global competitiveness is not simply inherited but must be created by the employers and employees of an economy and must be defended daily. The most successful economies in recent years are not those which are blessed with large natural resources such as minerals and rich farming land, but countries such as Japan, Switzerland and Germany, which lack rich natural resources. These countries have all earned their wealth by hard work, developing and applying modern technology and the high qualifications of their workers. The lack of natural resources necessitated innovative feats of labour. The efficient utilization of raw materials and the application of new materials has greatly reduced the competitive importance of natural resources. The sinking prices for raw materials in recent years proves this. Exploitation is no longer the problem of developing countries; the accelerated speed of technological innovation is. Such high speed innovation devalues capital and labour ever more rapidly and demands ever increasing investments. The ability to create innovative technologies and products has long become the decisive competitive criterion.

STAGNANT SOCIETIES ARE DOOMED

As long as a country maintains the lead in the technological race, its size is unimportant for its international competitiveness. Not only are companies competing, but societies as well. Flexibility and adaptability are social resources which must be created politically in the battle of opinions. Due to the acceleration of technological development, stagnant, *status quo* societies no longer have a chance to maintain or even increase their wealth. For these societies, the single market will have a rejuvenating and refreshing effect. It will break up old, sluggish structures and force the member countries to face new, or frequently suppressed, challenges which must be solved and can no longer be ignored.

Europe is an old continent with many national traditions and regional specialities. The charming side of this cultural abundance must naturally be preserved, but it has also accumulated a lot of dust which must be forcibly removed. The general euphoria connected with the new beginning makes it hard for special interest groups to maintain their *status quo*. National politics are entrenched in a quagmire of lobbies which prevent changes. Brussels, however, still has the chance to start anew. This is possible as the lobbies have not yet established themselves in European politics and the European parliament still has strictly limited power. Neither will remain so. Neither is supposed to. But European politics currently offers more freedom than anywhere else, even if the capitals think otherwise. Even national politicians are quite thankful that internal political barricades can be overcome with a little help from Brussels. The European Community is often held responsible for things which had to be done anyway.

INVENTIONS CANNOT BE PLANNED

The development of a new product is not a predictable process which begins in research laboratories, develops into a prototype and, more or less, automatically becomes marketable with a high turnover. Information technology, biotechnology, new materials and flexible production methods are without doubt important technologies which will create new markets, perhaps even new technologies. Their most important effect, however, has been that they have drastically changed many well-known products and production methods. As a result, all manufacturers and many service sectors have been affected by these new technologies. All must integrate them into their products and production methods if they intend to stay in the market. The development, production and application of new technologies in order to improve product quality has become a never-ending task for all industries – a task which has had a number of consequences for other branches. Accordingly, businesses must conduct total technology management. This management should concentrate not only on high-tech production methods and distribution channels, but also on the qualifications of the employees. Innovation is a collective term which consists of more than just technology, and it would be wrong to expect too much from high technology.

A sectoral industrial policy which only supports branches with good growth expectations by subsidies or trade barriers will not have much effect. It would be too simplistic to cope with the complex interaction of high-tech and global business strategies. Economic growth does not appear automatically if one has the right industries. Modern industries will thrive in one country or region and stagnate in another because it lacks qualified workers, a supplier infrastructure or stimulating competition.

... BUT THE GOVERNMENT IS ALSO RESPONSIBLE

I cannot see a direct correlation between high technology and competitiveness. International competitiveness is always a product of several factors of which some can be influenced decisively by industrial policy. Governments do not only create the framework; they are also actively involved in the economy, as suppliers and consumers of wares and services, as regulators and money lenders. Concentrating a nation's strengths for international competition is also an important part of industrial policy. No business can stand alone in today's global competition. The government has a lot to say on, for example, the number of school graduates, ie, the number of future workers, or the number of university graduates, or which type of public telecommunications network system will be available for the development of new services. The competitiveness of an economy can only be maintained by both industry and government.

LEARNING FROM THE JAPANESE

Japanese companies have demonstrated how to use micro-electronics in various branches of industry to develop new products and to revolutionize production methods. They have been highly successful in the mass production of electronic components of previously expensive or unwieldy products for professionals. Mass production made these products available to the masses. The inexpensive beginner models have especially made the term 'Made in Japan' famous the world over. The reputation of manufacturing low quality products disappeared long ago. This feat is not only a result of great marketing but of consequent improvement and adaptation of production methods. The integration of new controlling systems in flexible production processes has created a new branch of industry, robot systems, in which the Japanese now have a substantial global lead. Robot systems have also completely changed production methods in many branches of Japanese industry, making them the world's leader in quality.

European manufacturers are also good at continuously improving quality and production methods. The German machinery industry is an excellent example of the ability of continuous innovation. The 'inventor' mentality of the Swabian manufacturers has made them world famous. Gradual improvements are quite often more important in machinery than large breakthroughs. Small steps can also add up to a totally new machine. Traditional textile and printing machines have become high-tech products, which are built by the same German companies as the preceding machines. These German companies are world leaders and are thus responsible for returning to Germany jobs which had been lost to cheap-wage countries. The increasing capital intensity has reduced the importance of wage costs. New materials and flexible production processes have suddenly given traditional branches of industry such as the ceramics and textile industries (on which many observers in the 'developed' industrial nations of Europe had given up), new market chances.

IS EUROPE LOSING THE TECHNOLOGY RACE?

These positive examples should not make us ignore the fact that important indicators of technology are no longer very favourable for Europe. Statistics for Europe, the US and Japan about money spent on new technology and its application show that Europe still has to catch up on a lot of technology. The OECD statistics show that the amounts spent on research and development in Japan and the US are almost 3 per cent of the national product. This is one and a half times the amount spent in Europe, where it is less than 2 per cent of the national product. Only Germany spends about the same amount as Japan and the US. Research has become increasingly important in France, Italy and Holland since the beginning of the 1970s but it has not yet gained ground decisively. Europe is also far in the rear when comparing per capita expenditure on research. In 1989, Japan invested ECU 632 per capita on research and the US, ECU 478. Average European per capita expenditure was only ECU 274. Only Germany spent ECU 502, roughly the American amount. Italy spent ECU 177, Great Britain ECU 292, Holland ECU 297 and France ECU 360, putting these countries in last place. Europe also has a technological deficiency in the number of research engineers and scientists. Here, surprisingly, even Germany is much worse than Japan and the US.

Japan has a clear global lead in the use of robots. In Japan, there are 12 robots per 1,000 workers in those industries which can principally employ them. This is six times the European amount and even eight times that in the US. Although Germany has slightly more robots (2.7) than its European neighbours, this does not alter the fact that the leading European industrial nations are far behind Japan in this sector. Japan has gained this huge global lead in the application of robots by hard work and is now the world's leader in automation technology. As a result, Japan's productivity has increased much faster than in other industrial nations in recent years. The quality of its products has improved drastically as well. The low frequency of repairs in Japanese cars is the result of a globally unsurpassed application of industrial robots in the Japanese car industry.

The Japanese can produce a wide variety of types and in large numbers by the increasing application of automated machines. As a result, costs are lower, quality is higher, development is faster and the workers are more motivated. The advantages of this new production philosophy are clear but they cannot be simply copied. Classic mass production has become obsolete. The introduction of flexible production methods, however, requires a new relationship between companies and their employees, something which has yet to be practised in Europe. It will soon be difficult to differentiate between white- and blue-collar workers, something neither employers nor unions have completely realized yet. Related trade actions appear slightly out-of-date and dull. Wholesale reduction of working time no longer fits into a time where qualification is the limiting factor and costs are influenced more strongly by the amount of time machines are working rather than wages. New possibilities for pay-rate policies arise but new considerations also arise which may not be ignored.

Patents say a lot about the state of a country's technological development. From 1985 to 1988, more than 40 per cent of the world's patents, which were registered in more than one country, came from one of the European Community states. The US has roughly 28 per cent and Japan about 23 per cent of all international patents. This shows that Europe still has a high innovative potential, at least for the early stages of new technological development. Germany has roughly 15 per cent of all international patents. The high percentage of Europe's patents is slightly overestimated by the fact that patents which are registered in two or three European countries are considered international. The large domestic markets of Japanese and American companies do not force them to register international patents to the same extent as companies of other countries. Nevertheless, the situation of European companies concerning patents in the so-called future technologies is really not so bad. In communication and information technology, Europe's 26 per cent of the international patents are less than Japan's (43 per cent) but at the same level as America's. In biotechnology, Europe has 31 per cent in comparison to America's 42 per cent and Japan's 18 per cent. In environmental technology, however, Europe is the world's undisputed leader with 48 per cent, far ahead of the US (22 per cent) and Japan (12 per cent). In all three fields, Germany has more patents than any of its European neighbours. Germany is especially dominant in environmental technology with 29 per cent of all international patents. This shows how advantageous it was that Germany began its progressive environmental policy much earlier than any of its competitors.

DO WE NEED A TECHNOLOGICAL OFFENSIVE?

What conclusions for industrial policy can be drawn from the data concerning the technological competitiveness of European industry in comparison to its main rivals, Japan and the US? First of all, it must be emphasized that the data show a complex picture. Whereas the patent statistics indicate that Europe's industry still has a sound position in basic research, the other indicators show Europe to have lost much ground, especially in comparison to Japan. Obviously, Europe can still hold its own in basic research but threatens to lose contact with the top in the opening of future markets and in the application of modern and powerful production technology. This is where a European technological policy must act. It is now of primary importance that Europe's technical and scientific know-how is used to develop marketable products. Previously, the European Community concentrated mainly on basic research. This cannot be a dogma for all time, as technological knowledge is increasingly related directly to production technology itself.

The question for Europe's technological policy must be: how can new technologies be best promoted? The European Community spends roughly DM 65 billion on agriculture each year, but only about DM 12 billion are spent on basic research. The only specific research programme the European Community participates in currently is 'Eureka'. The Eureka project was founded in 1985 by the European Community, the EFTA countries and Turkey in order to regain ground lost to the Japanese and Americans in the field of high technology by joint research. More than 450 Eureka projects are supported with a total of DM 16 billion. The most well-known projects are Jessi (the development of 64-megabit memory chips), HDTV (high-definition television) and Prometheus (the development of a car of the future). There is no lack of European future-oriented projects. The deficiency is more apt to be in the determination of the European partners to conduct joint research. There are also fundamental objections against such sectoral-oriented support for technology, so-called 'picking up the winners' support, which cannot be easily denied.

It cannot be expected that governments are better than others at identifying 'strategic' technologies which will have the next technological breakthrough. Strategic support of research is always conducted with the tacit expectation that this will enable the supporting country, in this case the European Community, to become the world's leader in this field. The world has produced few successful cases in support of this theory. Usually, technology develops differently from the way official planning would have it occur. Even Japan, which is said to have had the most success with this strategic 'targeting' and whose economic prosperity is said to be based on this method, has had little success. Notwithstanding its determined efforts, Japan has not been able to create an internationally competitive chemical, pharmaceutical or aircraft industry. It also initially neglected the developments in the microcomputer market. A 'garage-based' company such as Apple showed the world the technical and commercial potentials of personal computers. Not a single 'technology' politician in the world had foreseen it.

EVEN MITI CAN BE MISTAKEN

I think the role of the legendary MITI, the Japanese Ministry for International Trade and Industry, as the nerve centre and secret control centre of the Japanese economy is very exaggerated. Its misses, chance hits and decisive successes roughly cancel each other out. This is very similar to the situation in an uncontrolled market. I am not denying that this ministry holds a large share of the responsibility for Japan becoming the third largest economic power in the world. However, the growing global involvement of Japanese companies has resulted in them taking less notice of the goals of MITI. Increasingly, Japanese companies follow their own strategy and are competing against each other in the world market. Industrial policy must allow this freedom, as otherwise mistakes will accumulate (the 'lemming effect') and soon negate the advantages. This is especially true for European companies which will not allow themselves to be forced into a European 'corset' of indicative planning or even informal agreements. Each business is much too concerned with its independence and self-reliance.

Large European companies see each other primarily as rivals and not as partners. Their interest in joint research programmes with the rest of the Community to regain lost technological ground is accordingly low. In principle, every company working in the same market is a competitor, and this, due to the former segmentation of the European market, is almost always the case. This closely limits European research cooperations. Sector-specific support programmes often fail because it is hardly sensible to distinguish between high and low technology any longer. Although new technologies do develop in some industries more often than in others, there is hardly a branch of industry which cannot apply new technologies at all. The revolution in micro-electronics has touched almost every industrial sector. Semi-conductors are employed in a range of products from various branches. Even biotechnology will result in a multitude of innovations in branches which few would connect immediately with high technology, namely the food and luxury food industry or in modern materials. Even the steel industry, on which many had already given up, has become high-tech with its modern production facilities. Shipbuilding now uses almost as much modern technology in its products as the aircraft industry.

HORIZONTAL STRENGTHENING OF COMPETITIVENESS

These facts show that the amount of research-intensive export goods says little about the actual competitive strength of a country. Statistics show that commodities with a medium amount of new technologies, such as cars and chemical products, are more important for the current account than, for example, video recorders, computers or modern materials. Consequently, technological policies should primarily improve conditions for innovations on a broad basis. A balanced variety of industrial branches with several second and third places is more important than a few isolated islands of high technology which are barely able to survive.

... by reducing capital costs

The development and application of new technologies is a gradual process which is characterized by trial and error. Enterprises must decide on introducing new products and production methods by themselves. They are also the first to realize whether a new technology is a dead-end or deserves more funding. Consequently, they must be able either to cut their losses quickly and flexibly or conduct a joint venture with non-European partners. In order to assume this responsibility for themselves, enterprises primarily need favourable sources of finance. The research and development costs for 256-kilobit memory chips were 100 million dollars. The corresponding costs for the 1-megabit chip are estimated to be 1 billion dollars. A main difficulty for European companies in conducting high-tech research and the consequent development of competitive products is undoubtedly the higher capital costs in comparison to Japan. High expenditures for research and development result in high funding needs. The higher capital intensity of production naturally plays a large role in these funding requirements – a logical result of the increase in production automation. However, increasing demands on the cleanliness of production, for example in the production of semi-conductor chips or in the reduction of downtime of machines or plants, lead to higher investment costs. Industry is increasingly requesting subsidies for production. Several European high-tech companies simply do not have the money to pay for facilities for the expensive production of chips.

The traditionally low real rate of interest in Japan is very advantageous for the funding of investment projects for Japanese companies. In the second half of the 1980s, interest rates were, on average, roughly 1 per cent lower in Japan than in Europe or the US. This is a considerable starting advantage for Japanese companies which have a high amount of funding by debt. Long-term planning is alleviated by this low real rate of interest and the close links between 'associated' companies and banks, something which is typical for Japan. Large investments also become profitable much more quickly. A deregulation of the Japanese financial system would lead to more equality in the ability to obtain funding but would not necessarily change the conditions at which Japanese banks loan money to 'their' companies. This makes it very important that European governments and central banks ensure low real rates of interest by responsible economic policies. Tax benefits for research and development could also result in advantageous financing. These horizontal solutions are preferable to sectoral subsidies, ie, public funds allocated by government officials, as these benefit all innovative companies.

... by simplifying the transfer of technology

The closer new technologies are to the market the more cautious a government should be with financial aids for single projects. In these cases general advantageous conditions for research and development are more important. This last stage is much more decisive than basic research. What makes successful nations successful is the fact that they are better at making marketable products of new technologies. This includes the ability to discover and open completely new markets for new technological applications. A very good example is the extraordinary and unexpected growth rate of telefacsimile (fax) devices. The Japanese companies which currently dominate the market discovered this gap in the telecommunication market a few years ago and they were able to bridge the gap with existing technological know-how. Other new technologies never make the market because commercial aspects were not taken into consideration early enough. Even the best car in the world could not be sold if, for instance, the trunk was too small. Customers want to use cars for transportation and not as show pieces – a fact that is occasionally forgotten in technological enthusiasm.

In the stage of commercial application of new technologies an active policy of technological transfer is especially important for small- and medium-sized companies, which cannot afford extensive research and development departments which would have an overview of all relevant new technologies. They need free access to data bases, patent search facilities and the research results of universities and scientific institutes. This is a special responsibility for chambers and associations of trade, as well as universities and other public institutions. Last but not least, large companies should allow small- and medium-sized companies to participate in new developments, especially when these companies serve as their suppliers. This is in their own interest, as they are dependent upon an efficient network of suppliers.

... by innovative government policies

The state as customer for high-quality technology plays an important role in the technological policy of companies. Unfortunately, governments are rarely demanding customers, as demonstrated by the uniform architecture of public buildings. A close look reveals the amount of dust that has also gathered inside these buildings. When awarding public contracts for office automation and telecommunication, governments have rarely been pioneers in technological innovations, even though the sheer quantity of governmental demand alone could provide a technological stimulus. Fast and courageous decisions could make governments pioneers in several areas of infrastructure. The integration of traffic, energy and telecommunication networks within the European Community requires an investment in high-quality technology in order to achieve the most efficient solutions for traffic and the distribution of energy. Courageous and future-oriented decisions in infrastructure would give the industry a huge technological stimulus, as proven by the French TGV and the German ICE. Governments also play a very important role in the development of demanding technologies in environmental areas. Strict standards and requirements do not hurt industry if they also lead to the development and application of modern technologies, for example, for the reduction of emissions or energy consumption. Governments cannot make business decisions better than the companies themselves. It is the task of governments to define public goals as early and clearly as possible so that industry can prepare for the new situation as early as possible. Governments have more than enough responsibilities so, if money is spent, they should demand as much in return as possible.

... by supporting training and continuing education

New technologies are not only used by an elite group of scientists and engineers, they are also used in one form or another by practically every worker. No one will dispute the fact that we can only keep up in the technological race if we have excellent scientists and engineers. This, however, is not sufficient. The general education of all other workers is just as important. Today, most offices are equipped with personal computers and text processing systems and, where this is not the case, it is only a matter of time until they are. New developments in telecommunications will ensure that offices continue to change in the future. Factories are increasingly being equipped with robots, numerically controlled machines and integrated, flexible production systems. Workers must receive their qualifications to use this equipment as early as possible. Education influences highly the acceptance of new technologies. The result is the willingness to plan and request the use of these technologies instead of a passive reaction to change. The dual system of education in Germany has been highly successful in this respect. It has ensured the high level of education of blue- and white-collar workers and continually adapts to new technological developments. Unfortunately, other members of the European Community are not of the same opinion concerning the importance of education, something that may become a severe locational disadvantage. Even substantial regional subsidies cannot persuade a technologically demanding industry to move to a region if it does not have the qualified workers it requires.

Demographic developments can lead to a Community-wide deficiency in qualified workers in the next few years. The smaller number of young workers joining the labour force will make re-education and continuing education more important than ever. The European Community cannot compete as a low-wage region. The expectations of its citizens are much too high and its social security too expensive. Consequently, in order to increase productivity, more young people in the Community must be persuaded to study technical and scientific subjects and to receive a practical education. Industry and government must create these necessary training facilities jointly. Employers must make education more attractive for the employees. Education is becoming less and less a matter only for young people; the high speed of technical progress requires that all workers remain willing to obtain new qualifications. There will be less and less 'simple' work available in the Community, but this only seems to bother few, for otherwise a European network for vocational training and continuing education would have been established long ago. Some are fighting about competence, others about money. Both must be overcome in order to devise a European solution which will finally offer workers in the European Community the same job opportunities. If not, high technology will be limited to few regions of the Community.

TAKING ADVANTAGE OF NATIONAL STRENGTHS

Technical ability, scientific knowledge, and a well-trained work force – these important production factors are not available for free. This is the essence of my convictions. The original availability of these factors is of less importance for the competitiveness of a country than the rate and speed with which these factors are created, improved and applied to a certain branch of industry. It is not enough simply to create favourable conditions for industry. Joint institutions between the government and industry, which make these advantages dynamic, are much more decisive. The dual educational system in Germany is a good example. Training courses are jointly defined and adapted to technological changes by government, industry and unions. This ensures that vocational education is always kept up to date. A discussion without prejudices about the relationship between politics and industry is frequently disturbed by the MITI syndrome. The Japanese model is truly not a standard for European industrial policy, as it is too closely related to the Japanese culture and society and, consequently, cannot be transferred to Europe. Europeans have neither the group mentality nor the need for mutual agreement which would be necessary to get European industry to accept a common purpose without government force. However, Europeans will not be able to avoid an increased adjustment of their interests and learning to use their strengths more efficiently.

This does not mean that the locational advantages of a country are to be destroyed. These advantages must be totally preserved in the single market. Each country must develop its strengths to the fullest extent. Its weaknesses will, hopefully, be gradually removed by the competition in the single market. Germany's strength is, for example, technology. Germany tends to be a producing society, with high savings, technically educated managers, and excellently qualified workers. There are many similarities to Japan. Germany's weaknesses are in the service sector and consumer products. The single market will result in many changes, from a wider variety of services to a liberalization of shop closing times.

Italy's strengths are the well-known ability to improvise and the flexibility of its numerous small family enterprises, which are very successful in filling economic niches. Government institutions are primarily weak. The single market will help correct this. Missing national standards and quality standards are being defined at the European level. This will be especially advantageous for countries previously lacking a bureau of standards with an international reputation. The economic and monetary union will also necessitate more government discipline. The fear of not being a first class European country will hopefully result in enough reforms to balance state budgets and create modern governments.

Great Britain's specific part in strengthening Europe is its service sector, for example, banks, insurances and advertising, which are world leaders in their field. Strong British efforts have ensured that insurance companies will not be limited to a single country in the Community and that comparative advertisement will be permitted. Speculative forces can also damage the industrial basis of a country. When managers are forced to worry about takeovers and unproductive defence strategies, business will suffer sooner or later. This seems to be a British weakness. The single market will also help here by clearly defining conditions under which companies may be taken over. These conditions will help capital mobility but not pure speculation. We do not want to sell Europe to the highest bidder; we want to strengthen its industrial competitiveness.

France's strength is surely the strategic and occasionally visionary thinking of its leaders. This will be an important corrective measure against all too blind trust in the powers of the market. It is naturally possible to buy chips in Japan. The more ambitious goal is producing them in Europe to avoid technological dependence. The single market shows that it is not possible to create external barriers and that international competition cannot be avoided. In this manner, each country can learn something from the other. European industrial policy is also the attempt to free the European economies from their ideological stagnation. Planned economies are certainly not competitive in today's complex market. The market, however, cannot do everything by itself. Strong, social institutions and structures are also needed to systematically drive technological progress, improve qualifications and maintain social consent. The Commission understands itself to be a moderator and not a manipulator. European industrial policy wants to pose the right questions, but the answers must be primarily given by others. The main object of industrial policy is the willingness to adapt and that cannot be bought with government money.

5

The Industrial Policy Stimulus of Open Borders

No industrial country can maintain external barriers if it wants to stay competitive and preserve its wealth. The increasing globalization of the economy has created a world without economic borders in which only vocational qualifications and the ability to live with structural changes decide over the future of a country or region. In this global market where companies are able to select production locations with the best competitive advantages, independent of national origin, it is completely hopeless to try to force foreign companies out of a market by industrial policy or try to protect domestic businesses. Import barriers and tariffs can be overcome by direct investments, regulations concerning 'local content' can be circumvented by creating a network of suppliers and reciprocity clauses, which make imports dependent upon one's exports, can be avoided by buying up domestic industries.

UTILIZING THE GLOBAL MARKET OFFENSIVELY

The world market has a counter-measure for every protectionist move. It is impossible to run away from global competition: sooner or later, someone will be faster, no matter how fast one can run. In the race between the hare and the tortoise, protectionism always loses in the long run. Nevertheless, some governments and enterprises invest much time and energy avoiding international competition instead of attacking in time. Thus, much time and political goodwill are wasted with useless evasive tactics before fate and competition are accepted.

Global competition must not be seen primarily as a danger against which European industry must defend itself. Quite often the more powerful trading partners are held responsible for the mistakes and deficiencies of domestic industrial policy. This attitude is short-sighted and much too defensive. It can be seen the other way around: international competition is simultaneously a warning and a teacher, which will uncover weaknesses in time to correct them. Consequently, creating and maintaining international competition is the best industrial policy possible. Only an open, competitive environment forces companies to keep working on and upgrading products to adapt to new customer demands. The stimulus of the world market could not be replaced by anything else. For this reason, the single market should not become a 'closed shop' to non-European companies.

THERE IS NO REASON TO FEAR A 'EUROPEAN FORTRESS'

The appeal for open borders is more than just words, it also governs our behaviour in industrial policy. Facts have proven fears that the single market could result in a 'European fortress' to be wrong. The repetition of these fears is based more on strategy than on actual fear that the removal of internal borders and trade barriers within the Community could be accompanied by the creation of external trade barriers. There are no signs for this. The single market will be more easily available to our trading partners than twelve separate markets. Demands for trade barriers will appear time and time again, but where will they not? Europe's historic connections with the rest of the world are much too close for the European Community to hide behind trade barriers. Europe's traditional lead in world trade also contradicts this. Europe's citizens would not tolerate such a policy anyway. Europe is and will remain the largest and most open market in the world.

An open market for external trade partners is the logical balance to the single market. As long as the trade policy of the European Community is not harmonized, member countries will still be able to limit the amount of imports from outside the Community, something which the various countries use to varying extents. A well-known example is the import quota set for Japanese cars. This will be discussed in more detail later. There are numerous other national limits as well. The completion of the single market will make purely national limits of this type worthless, as it will no longer be possible to limit imports via internal borders. Such quotas would have to be extended to the whole Community to remain effective as a protection from foreign competition, but there is no chance that this could happen. The Commission would have been completely misguided to let national quotas be extended to cover those countries of the Community which had previously had more or less open borders. Quite the opposite: trade barriers must be removed and not extended. At the most, a transition time to the complete opening could be permitted which would allow adaptation to these open borders. Affected companies would thus receive a little more time for adaptive business measures. This would enable problems to be solved which could prove unresolvable in shorter periods of time.

THE AGRICULTURAL POLICY OF THE EC MAKES IT UNTRUSTWORTHY

The protectionism of the EC agricultural policy is the main source of trade policy irritations with our partners. It does give reason to doubt the European sincerity concerning open borders. Closing our borders to agricultural products also robs us of our arguments for opening foreign borders for our machines, cars and aircraft, especially as many jobs in these branches depend directly or indirectly on exports. Global exports are the basis for the competitiveness of these and other industries. Without exports, the sales numbers required for low sales prices and to finance the enormous research and development activities could not be achieved. 'Europe for the Europeans' would surely mean the end for many export companies. Even the large single market would be too small to achieve production scales which would be profitable. This is more important than just the risk of not selling one or two cars or aircraft in a foreign country. The European Community is a conglomeration of twelve countries whose wealth is based on an efficient industry. We are risking this basis by our expensive protectionism for agricultural products.

A fundamental reform of the European agricultural policy is long overdue. It is a policy based on protectionism; it is inefficient and unsocial. No one is happy with it: the producers because their subjective income expectations are not met by the government time and time again; the consumers because they pay for the over-priced products twice – once when buying them and again when paying increased taxes. Other producers of agricultural products are justly incensed that their competitive products are forced from the world market by export-subsidized goods from the European Community. It is not enough that the European Community blocks agricultural imports, its subsidized exports ruin world market prices and the chances of others to earn foreign exchange. All these problems are well known and still nothing changes.

THE TARGET IS TO ELIMINATE SURPLUS AGRICULTURAL PRODUCTION

It must become the most important goal of reform to reduce surplus agricultural production in the Community. The larger the reduction, the smaller the export pressure and the higher agricultural prices will be. Current world market prices cannot be the only goal for agricultural product prices within the European Community, as our own subsidized exports substantially distort world market prices downwards. The elimination of surplus production would result in normal market conditions under which prices are dictated by demand. This would especially help those European farmers who want to be free farmers and not socially subsidized producers. They are still far away from this goal. They currently produce mainly for EC storage bins and not for the market. The donation of these storage surpluses to the former Soviet Union or the Third World cannot be considered a long-term solution to this problem.

Protectionism does not really protect farmers much either. Supposedly, we are protecting small- and medium-sized farms. However, 80 per cent of the subsidies are spent on only 20 per cent of the farms, mostly those who could survive anyway. Surprising as it may seem, it is possible to convince the farmers of exactly the opposite. As a result, farmers demonstrate, with occasionally murderous slogans, for an agricultural policy which does not help them at all. It would be much more sensible to help small- and medium-sized farms by direct income aids and to finance programmes to shutdown further agricultural areas. This would result in a transient increase in subsidies required to compensate losses due to market-oriented prices. However, the subsidies would at least go where they are supposed to and not end up somewhere else. An agricultural policy which, by inflated prices, creates a surplus that must then be subsidized to be sold on the world market, is doomed to eventual failure. Additional agricultural countries,

Hungary and Poland for example, will most probably have joined the Community by the turn of the century. The surplus problem will then become even worse if nothing is done. That is the latest date at which the current agricultural system with its refund prices, variable import/export levies and export reimbursements will collapse. Is this what will have to happen before the European Community reforms its agricultural policy?

PROTECTIONISM HURTS EVERYBODY

Protectionism also hurts industry more than it helps. Recent experience shows whoever wants to know that protective measures for single industries have only rarely increased their competitiveness. This is not really surprising. When an industry knows that its products have a safe market which is protected from competitors, it tends to relax and ignore those difficult foreign markets. Protective measures are only acceptable if their duration is strictly limited and their transitory character is obvious. The most successful global industries are not those with the most restrictive import regulations and the highest levies, but those which are most strongly exposed to international competition. Anything else leads, sooner or later, to worse products and, consequently, lower sales figures. Governments are much more easily convinced of the necessity of national protective measures than customers who, luckily, do the final judging in an economy. The roots and not the symptoms must be fought when international competitiveness is lacking. This cannot be repeated often enough.

... THEREFORE THE GATT TRADE TALKS MUST NOT BE ALLOWED TO FAIL

The agricultural policy of the European Community has made itself the target for trade policy complaints, although other countries are not as innocent as they would like to appear, for example Japan with its prohibition of rice imports. The stubbornness of the European Community has made it easy for its critics to step out of the limelight themselves. The original goal of the GATT (General Agreement on Tariffs and Trade) trade talks was to eliminate agricultural subsidies which distort competition and especially export reimbursements. Important negotiating parties have drifted ever further from this goal and now demand the total abolition of agricultural subsidies. This, however, is not only unacceptable, it is also not sensible, as agricultural subsidies could help reduce surplus production and its negative effect in the world market. By its lack of flexibility in agricultural questions, Europe has lost the chance to complain more about its partners' hidden trade barriers. These invisible import barriers still impede trade and services much more than levies and import quotas, because the latter are at least obvious and predictable. This only emphasizes the necessity of multilateral agreements to reduce all types of trade barriers and to finally create fair rules for global trade which are respected by all trading countries. GATT must stop being a 'sheriff without a jail' as it was once called. The enforceability of GATT rules must be increased. Regulations which can be broken with impunity are soon ignored.

International trade is a fragile system, comparable with a game of dominoes. The single domino can endanger the whole system. Every one who is willing to break GATT rules to gain a small advantage or who is unwilling to allow more stringent application and enforceability of these rules should know this. There is an increasing tendency to bilateralism in trade policy. Nothing can be said against two or more trading partners meeting regularly to solve current irritations and problems jointly. This method was extremely useful for standards. Free trade can only profit when both sides agree to use international standards in public requests for bids and to mutually recognize each other's test certificates to avoid costly double testing. Such bilateral talks can only be warmly approved of. The same is true for regional cooperations, such as the creation of the free trade zone from Alaska to Mexico or the close cooperation of the ASEAN countries. It cannot be approved of if two countries try to solve their problems to the disadvantage of a third. Japan and the US especially tend to such agreements. The most recent example is the extension of the semi-conductor agreement which diverts surplus capacities to other markets.

TRADE POLICY BILATERALISM IS A DEAD-END

The increase in trade policy bilateralism is the result of a lack of confidence in the success of the general GATT rules and also the attempt to give only as much as absolutely necessary. Bilateral talks are naturally compromises in which neither party asks too much of the other. Difficult problems are excluded or covered up by declarations of intent which always stay well under the pain threshold. As such, the Japanese always promise to open their markets and the Americans promise to reduce their budget and current account deficits which raise interest rates all over the world. Nevertheless, these declarations are not binding and are thus repeated anew each year. The GATT system, however, is the unique attempt to achieve free trade by rules which apply to all and which are not a diplomatic compromise on some distribution formula. Free trade is not based on equal results but on equal chances. This basic principle of free trade is very much endangered if he who did not or could not use a chance, is able to correct the result by negotiation.

This increasing tendency to solve problems bilaterally creates a difficult situation for the European Community. Free trade will never receive a chance once countries believe that protectionism pays off. European companies can expect the European Community to protect their interests in the same manner as the American and Japanese governments do for their industries. It is unimportant whether the complaints are justified or not. When politics replaces the market, trade flow is no longer determined by companies in markets but by bureaucrats in international conferences. It is not surprising that countries with long traditions in diplomacy trust this method of negotiation more than anonymous market forces which cannot be influenced politically. Demanding a result-related balance of trade flow, ie, reciprocity in its strictest sense, makes global trade a poker game with a risky finish. Closing borders becomes a tactical means of forcing economic concessions.

When everybody starts violating the principles of free trade, the European Community will be forced to participate. Who will be willing to sacrifice the interests of European industries for principles which are violated all the time? Countries must know this when they prefer to sign bilateral agreements instead of strengthening GATT rules. It just shows that they do not quite trust the abstract principles of free trade after all. This is not a threat, it is a warning. It is difficult for those convinced of free trade to praise the advantages of open borders when new barriers are being created everywhere and old barriers are being defended with all means available. Here again, the basic problem is communications. GATT talks have almost become a routine occurrence at the civil service level. The personal engagement of political leaders is missing – something which made the talks possible in the first place. Multinational talks must develop a dynamic of their own to become successful. For GATT, this seems to have been lost in the narrow-minded arguments over agricultural subsidies. The most important prerequisite for a successful conclusion to the GATT talks seems to be reviving the 'spirit of Punta del Este', the coastal bathing resort in Uruguay where the GATT talks of 1987 were initiated.

FREE TRADE AND ANTI-DUMPING ARE TWO SIDES OF THE SAME COIN

For all the trust in the achievements of international agreements concerning the reduction of trade barriers, effective instruments for the fight against unfair trading practices are still very necessary. Effective anti-dumping measures are the other half of opening markets. The European Community must retain this option to combat firmly dumping which could ruin the market. Unfortunately, some countries try again and again to increase their share of the world market by low-price strategies and so increase their exchange proceeds. This strategy, however, ruins stable and efficient market structures. In the interest of European industry, this cannot be tolerated. Frequently, the threat of anti-dumping measures is enough to frighten away potential wrongdoers. This alone would justify its existence. It is important that the use of such measures be transparent to all. The stronger partner must not always be able to force the weaker partner to accept its interpretation of the rules. It is not always dumping when a product is sold for less on a foreign market than at home. As in all cases of trade policy, the principle of appropriateness must be observed.

DO NOT OVERDO RECIPROCITY

A further danger for free world trade is the mistaken application of the principle of reciprocity in trade policy. Nothing can be said principally against reciprocity when meaning equal access to markets. Reciprocity, however, meaning sectoral trade balancing, ie, car for car, steel for steel or computer for computer, would in the end sacrifice the international division of labour and specialization. That would be the end of free trade, which is based on each country developing and applying its own strengths in the global division of labour. It is also wrong to give single, bilateral trade imbalances too much importance. If everyone were to demand trade surpluses with every country, international trade would come to a halt.

Reciprocity can only be justified in the sense of national treatment, ie, the legal equality of foreign and domestic companies. In this sense, the European Community is willing to give third-country banks licences for the whole single market if, on the other hand, EC banks are given the same rights as domestic banks in the applicant's country of origin. This is a very generous offer when one considers that, for example, the American market is highly subdivided and the registration of a bank in a single American state does not offer the same opportunities as registration in a member country of the Community. We cannot expect our banks to be able to operate all over the world according to European law. That would really be too much to expect. What we can expect, however, is that our banks are given the same rights as domestic banks, ie, the same chances for refinancing, the same opportunities and the same supervisory standards. There is not much that can be said against that.

'Equal rights for all' is the motto of free trade. This is the only way to save global free trade. Sectors where this principle is not yet completely realized, for instance services and public requests for bids, will require separate negotiations. Reciprocity clauses can be a sensible way to open doors for free global trade but not for limiting it. In such a case, its weakest member would determine how much trade would be permissible. Lacking interest in exports does not allow one to turn around and block foreign imports. No market is given to an exporter. Customers demand individual attention. Companies which consider this too much work, or which do not want to learn foreign languages or customs, should not be surprised if their own markets are more successfully exploited by others. The economic endurance test is presence in the most fought-over markets of the world. Companies who pass this test will also be successful in their domestic market.

DIRECT INVESTMENTS ARE NOT 'TROJAN HORSES'

Direct investments of foreign companies in the Community are very welcome. Creating research, production and sales facilities all over the world is just as much a part of the world economy as international trade. European companies invest far more in other continents than they invest in Europe. American companies began decades ago to create their own European production facilities or to participate in traditional European companies. American multinationals were the pioneers in global engagement and it is hard to imagine Europe without them. Some American companies are so integrated into Europe that they have almost become Europeans. It was only recently that the association of European car manufacturers accepted Ford and General Motors as members.

Japanese companies have also discovered the European market and have invested in European production facilities. These 'transplants' have naturally not yet taken root as well as the Americans. The normal procedure is that direct investments initially begin with the final assembly of pre-fabricated parts which are made in Japan. Independent development in the Japanese branches in Europe will follow later. Although nothing can be said against it, Japanese companies are often accused of investing in Europe only in order to circumvent tariffs, quotas and dumping levies. Japanese production facilities are called 'Trojan horses', as if we were conducting a trade war with Japan whose main object is national pride and not market shares. No one would stop to check where the headquarters of European companies are: subsidiaries are just as welcome as investors.

It makes sense for Japanese companies to begin with simple assembly line production before they transfer more demanding activities, such as the development and production of high quality components, to Europe. Taking the briefness of the Japanese engagement in Europe into consideration, it is also not surprising that these activities are not more extensive than they currently are. A trend to create independent product development centres in Europe and to increase cooperation with domestic companies is nevertheless apparent. In a few years, cars will not only be built in Japan and exported to Europe, but they will also be built in Europe and exported to the US or even Japan itself. Then finally, will these transplants be considered European companies.

DELIBERATION IS MORE IMPORTANT THAN NATIONALISM

The European industry also profits from direct Japanese investments in Europe, as Japanese production and, even more importantly, managerial methods are imported as well. The reason for the lead of Japanese companies in productivity is no secret; it is based on production methods which have been known since the 1960s. European arrogance has helped keep these reasons undiscovered and uncopied. Cooperation with Japanese companies could teach European suppliers how to continually refine products and how to deliver on time. Such experience would also be profitable for European industry. Japan has studied and copied much from the leading industrial nations in Europe and the US. Why should Europe not copy the more efficient Japanese production and managerial methods or, at least, conduct a comparison? European pride should not stand in the way.

In the long run, the subsidiaries of Japanese companies in Europe will become as European as the American subsidiaries already have. Consequently, there is absolutely no reason to discriminate against direct investments by Japanese or other non-European competitors. A company's country of origin must not decide the treatment it receives in Europe. Non-European companies which follow the rules of the Community must be allowed free access to the whole European Community. Nor must they be put at a disadvantage in regional policy. In this instance, the question, 'What is a Japanese company?' is totally irrelevant. In any case, it is becoming increasingly difficult to determine, as companies are making less and less themselves. Consequently, thinking in national categories is pointless. German cars will soon be as rare as Japanese cars, as more and more components are being built outside the country. These components are then only put together in Germany, Japan or another country. Even Europeans cannot ignore the resulting production reserves.

THERE IS AN EXCEPTION TO EVERY RULE

There are only three exceptions to these basic statements. First, we cannot tolerate that anti-dumping measures are circumvented by tightening the last screw of a pre-fabricated product in the European Community. These 'screwdriver' products must be treated in the same manner as products against which punitive levies have been imposed in accordance with GATT regulations. At least half of the value added, especially of the technically important components, must originate from European production in order to alleviate the suspicion of circumvention. Second, public contracts must be allowed to stipulate that European companies participate in an appropriate manner. This is the only possibility to protect European companies from competitive disadvantages and to put pressure on the mostly blocked purchasing markets of other countries. Opening these markets will not be easy, as many countries have given private businesses exclusive rights to public contracts. These private companies, however, are not required to request bids publicly. This must not result in competitive disadvantages for European companies. Finally, foreign companies must participate in research programmes financed by the European Community. Normally, such a participation is no problem whatsoever. Consequently, most European research programmes are open to non-European companies. Such generosity cannot apply, however, to strategic research areas in which European industry is still lagging behind. In these cases, research results are supposed to help European companies and not the international competition. Otherwise, we could use the money for something else. Businesses would hardly be willing to participate in a European research cooperation if, by doing so, they would be giving important company secrets to competitors working on the same project. This generosity is not available anywhere in the world and we do not need to have a bad conscience because of it.

Apart from these understandable exceptions, non-European companies have the same rights within the European Community as domestic companies. This is occasionally hard for various countries to understand, but according to the EEC treaties it is unimportant who owns a company as long as it is situated in the European Community. Foreign investments are completely safe in the European Community. The Commission has already proved that this is not an empty promise as, for example, in the case of the 'Blue Bird' which is produced in Great Britain by Nissan. This car may be sold without any limitations, including French import quotas on Japanese cars, in the whole Community. If necessary, the Commission would have enforced this by legal action resulting from the breach of contract. There must be no doubt that the freedom of movement for goods, services and capital is unlimited within the European Community.

THE GLOBAL APPROACH MEANS ACCEPTING THE JAPANESE CHALLENGE

Direct Japanese investments in Europe may not stay uni-directional. The European industry itself must do more to increase its presence in foreign markets, especially the Japanese market, for example, by having its own production facilities in these markets. This is the basic element of a global business strategy. It requires, however, that our companies are treated as fairly in Japan as Japanese companies are treated here. There is still a lot to do. The Commission will support companies wanting to invest in Japan as well as it can. We will not start applying reciprocal treatment to Japanese companies, but we will defend the interests of European investors to the best of our ability. This is part of an industrial policy which is based on opening markets. We will apply ourselves for our industry in the same manner in which the Americans apply themselves in Japan for Boeing and IBM, especially for more participation in government contracts.

Many are not very optimistic about the chances of opening closed markets, especially the Japanese. 'There is a further door behind each door' is the resigned statement of businesses which lost against the institutional particularities of Japan. There are, however, a few encouraging examples. German car manufacturers, for instance, were successfully able to create their own distribution networks in

Japan, or receive access to the frequently obscure Japanese distribution channels by cooperation with domestic sales companies. The German car manufacturers have been quite successful: they occasionally export cars of more total value to Japan than Japan exports to Germany. This must not be short-lived.

Although I do not believe that Japanese society will soon develop into a Western economy, I do believe that the increased integration of Japan into the world economy will gradually change the European Community as well. Even if it is only due to the fact that Japan no longer has anything to lose. The high Japanese trade surpluses have been profitably invested all over the world, in real estates, factories and patents. This increases the Japanese interest in multilateral treaties, as popular opinion highly endangers them in bilateral agreements. Not only the weak need others. The strong and powerful must worry about their wealth if the rules of free trade and capital movement are no longer respected and they can be hurt by one-sided sanctions. This mutual dependency is perhaps the best guarantee for the long-term victory of fairness over protectionism.

Part II

IDEAS FOR EUROPEAN INDUSTRIAL POLICY: FIVE EXAMPLES

Industrial policy is neither a nightmare nor a universal weapon in the fight for market shares and jobs. Perhaps we should, for this reason, avoid using this term and simply implement what we consider to be correct industrial policy. The term 'industrial policy' itself is hotly disputed within the individual member countries of the Community. 'European industrial policy' is, of course, an even better target for critics: it is insufficient for some, and it goes too far for others. We must do a lot of persuading in both directions before we can implement a reasonable industrial policy in the EC. European industrial policy must combine political necessities with sensible economics. Economically sound reasons alone often break down in the face of political realities. It is equally impossible, however, to assert realistic political ideas when confronted with economic resistance. They have to go hand in hand. By following what I consider a reasonable middle path between the ideological extremes of market glorification on the one hand and national authoritarianism on the other, European industrial policy occasionally ends up falling between both stools. However, neither blind faith in market economics nor political innocence will solve the current problems of industrial policy.

Pragmatism should not be confused with a lack of principles. In most cases, it is not simply a decision between a free market and statism, but it is rather a matter of creating or maintaining the competitive ability of European industry. The economic dogmatist, of course, would answer 'competition' when asked this question. What exactly does this mean? Does competition mean that market results must be accepted more or less as they come, even if it means the last European manufacturer is forced out of business? Or does competition also mean avoiding economic dependency and ensuring that there are as many suppliers as possible? As I understand it, European industrial policy should ignore neither the priority of international competitiveness nor the fact that not all of our competitors in the world market follow the rules of fair play. Industrial policy must, therefore, not only strengthen the competitive ability of European industry but also defend it against dominating competition. This is the distinguishing factor between European industrial policy and national strategies, which are blind in either one eye or the other.

European industrial policy is neither unperceptive nor naive. The basic concept was explained in great detail in the first part of this book. In the second part, I should like to illustrate the practical implications of this concept using a few selected examples. Each example represents an essential attribute of European industrial policy. The example of import quotas for Japanese cars shows the effects of protectionism and how it can be overcome by the single EC market. There was a long and rather heated discussion concerning this within the EC which produced an acceptable solution. Shipbuilding is an example of how a traditional sector of the economy can increase its competitive ability without assistance programmes or subsidies. The third example, aviation, represents a highly competitive industry of the future, but whose future will not drop like ripe fruit into our laps. The electronics industry is our hope for the future as well as our problem child. In this case, there is an especially fine line between an open market and government intervention. Electronics will determine which strategy for industrial policy will succeed in the EC. My last example, biotechnology and pharmacy, deals with a very special problem. In this case, the decisive challenge for industrial policy is gaining public acceptance. This calls less for public funding than for political courage, which is often even harder to find. These are all applied examples of everyday politics and are, therefore, best suited to illustrate the patchwork character of European industrial policy.

1

Quotas as a Sign of Weakness: The Motorcar Industry

The single market of the European Community would not be complete if certain sectors of the economy were excluded from the supporting principle of competition. This is especially true for the motorcar sector which, based on its share of the gross national product and the number of employees, plays a key role in the EC. The success of the single market greatly depends on the successful incorporation of this sector into the single market. It is also important that industrial policy allows the European car manufacturers to catch up with the Japanese competition. This will only be possible if they stand up to the international competition in the domestic markets.

A FREE SINGLE MARKET FOR CARS

A free single market for cars will be realized when the manufacturers can sell throughout the community with a single type approval and the European customer can choose whether he wants to buy his car in Copenhagen or in Flensburg, in Strasbourg or in Freiburg. This is not entirely possible at the moment. The technical type approval for motor vehicles is still based on various national regulations. There are also varying import restrictions into third countries which make it impossible for the customer to buy his car in any country he chooses. Nor are the dealers particularly helpful in this matter. Although the net prices for identical models differ greatly from country to country (not just as a result of the varying taxes which cannot be entirely passed on in some countries) there are comparatively few international car sales. The sales policy of the manufacturers is also partially to blame.

The elimination of customs will make it necessary to introduce a common type approval for motor vehicles and remove all national import restrictions. Great progress has already been made in harmonizing the technical regulations necessary for Community-wide vehicle registration. Of the 44 individual guidelines, 41 have been passed. Only the last three technical details are still being discussed by the advisory board. Trying to unify the guidelines using the old method of complete approximation of municipal laws and not by simply determining the basic safety requirements has proven to be a great disadvantage. The old method not only requires unanimity, but is also an extremely ponderous bureaucratic procedure, as is once again illustrated here. After the preliminary work at the department level had reached an advanced stage, the new process would have meant a great saving of time. The single market goal may not have been reached.

...AND THAT MEANS: NO MORE NATIONAL RESTRICTIONS

As long as EC regulations for cars are not uniform, national regulations apply. This includes technical regulations as well as national import restrictions, which still exist. Italy has had a bilateral car import treaty with Japan since the 1950s; it has never been terminated. Spain, France and Portugal also have traditionally autonomous import restrictions, some of which have been ratified by GATT. None of these, however, have been denied by Japan. Great Britain has an informal self-restriction agreement between her own and Japanese industry which is still used despite the fact that an increasing number of British cars are produced in Japanese factories. Other European manufacturers are justly angry about this practice. Protecting their own market and producing Japanese cars mainly for the continent is not fair play.

The intricate web of legal and half-legal import restrictions makes it difficult to create a single market for motor vehicles. Countries with legal import restrictions regularly apply for exemptions from open market principles within the Community according to paragraph 115 of the EEC treaty and countries without official import restrictions are constantly tempted to decrease the trade of goods within the community by imposing special technical controls or lengthy approval processes in order to stop the indirect import of Japanese cars through other member countries. This is not actually permitted, but has the same effect for potential buyers of Japanese cars as do legal import restrictions. The existing trade barriers within the single market can, theoretically, only be removed through legal action. The Commission has two possible methods to achieve this: authorized import restrictions could be ended simply by not granting any more exemptions according to paragraph 115 of the EEC treaty, and hidden import restrictions could be fought with actions for infringement of the treaty according to paragraph 30 of the EEC treaty. In especially discriminating cases, this is already being done. Often, however, the plaintiffs retract their complaints because they suddenly came to a settlement out of court or they no longer wish to fight the government. Many cases have fizzled out in this way. The legal process has often turned out to be a blind alley.

NO SINGLE MARKET FOR CARS BY BRUTE FORCE

The single market for cars could not have been realized by the end of 1992 through legal action alone. Action for infringement of the treaty is too time consuming and is not easy to win because the EC does not have the means to impose sanctions. A solution is difficult to enforce even within the framework of common trade policy. Rejecting applications for exemptions to paragraph 115 would have split the member countries into two parties: 'protectionists' on the one hand and 'free traders' on the other. A uniform type approval, the core of the single market, would then have been in danger of being blocked by the advisory board because the 'protectionists' on the advisory board probably would have refused to accept the necessary guidelines. There would have been only a lengthy political struggle with an uncertain outcome instead of the single market. It would not have been politically clever to use force to establish the single market in an area as important as the car industry.

The reason for eliminating national import restrictions is the elimination of customs. It can be argued that the member countries indirectly agreed to the elimination of national protective measures by agreeing to the elimination of customs, because the protective measures cannot be enforced without them. However, such intricately woven judicial arguments are of little use in everyday politics.

The EC may be a legal community but it also requires a basic political consensus; the common legal instruments are still too weak to enforce the single market when confronted with resistance from individual member countries.

... BUT VOLUNTARY SELF-LIMITATION IS A SOLUTION

In this situation, there is only one solution to the problem: voluntary self-limitation by the Japanese attached to the promise of a completely open market by 1999. This would establish the single market for cars immediately while allowing the protected industries, especially in France and Italy, enough time to adjust. The Japanese share of the market in the EC will only gradually increase – on average from the current 11 per cent to just 18 per cent at the end of the agreement. The increase on the currently protected markets, however, should be kept to a minimum to avoid large losses for local manufacturers. This was the most that could be achieved, even under market economy considerations. Nevertheless, it was possible to avoid a community quota; an informal monitoring of Japanese car imports, managed by the Japanese themselves, is enough.

Such a 'gentlemen's agreement' is certainly advantageous to both sides. It promises Japanese manufacturers a complete opening of the European market in the future without risking expensive trade conflicts which would damage their reputation. Nor is this a negligible agreement as the upper limit increases from year to year thereby allowing the market share for Japanese cars to increase as well. The EC car industry, on the other hand, gains time to adjust to the increased Japanese production level. If industry succeeds as well in this matter as we all hope, the Japanese market share may even be less than the upper limit agreed to. As we see, European manufacturers can help determine how many Japanese cars are sold within the EC. They must, however, use the time which has been given to them. There will probably not be another chance. At some point, the Japanese will no longer be willing to practise 'voluntary' self-limitation just because they build better cars (as this is definitely not a case of dumping).

A sudden removal of the import restrictions would have been neither politically possible nor justifiable in terms of industrial policy as it would most likely have led to the collapse of previously protected industries. According to a study by McKinsey, the Japanese would have approximately doubled their sales by the mid-1990s if they had open access to the European market. At the same time, sales by the major European manufacturers would have decreased dramatically, especially Fiat with 209,000 less cars sold annually, followed by Peugeot (with 190,000 less cars), Volkswagen (with 170,000 less cars) and Renault (with 156,000 less cars). As a result, 120,000 to 140,000 jobs would be lost. With such numbers, we need not have any illusions about the amount of space for political negotiations. It is not enough merely to encourage free trade, it must also be backed up politically. In this respect, there was hardly a realistic alternative to the method of Japanese self-limitation chosen by the Committee even if this intermediate measure is not entirely satisfactory. I can only agree to this solution because, at the end of the transitional period, the GATT rules will be fully accepted. We must now work towards this goal.

DECENCY WINS: A TRANSITIONAL SOLUTION

The competitive ability of European car manufacturers must be considerably improved in order to reach the goal of a complete open market after the transitional period. This will also cost jobs, but at least the necessary rationalization will not be made more difficult through large sales losses. Even so, there is not much time. If the negotiated transitional period is not used, parts of the European car industry will fall even further behind in international competition. There would not be competition and free trade in goods at the end of the transitional period, but rather protective measures that are even stronger than the relatively mild 'monitoring'.

The lesson to be learned here is that a strict competitive 'laissez-faire' policy in practice sometimes produces exactly the opposite of the desired goal. Abstaining from regulatory politics would not, in this case, necessarily lead to increased competition. It would, rather, cement the existing national import restrictions. Critics deliberately ignore this when they call the agreement a 'victory for protectionism'. Protectionism did not win, decency did. We must not underestimate the fact that, despite the transitional measures, freedom of movement for motorcars is going to be created immediately. From 1993, any car in the EC can be sold from anywhere to anywhere. There are definitely less restrictions than before, not more. The Commission did not create national import restrictions and they cannot be removed immediately either.

The first question relevant to industrial policy is now: What are the causes of the problems the European car industry is having? All car manufacturers must move within the boundaries of market potential and productivity. Market potential is determined by presence in the important markets, ie in the US, Europe and Japan, as well as in markets in the newly-industrialized and developing countries which will have the most dynamic growth in the years to come. Productivity, on the other hand, is determined by the manufacturer's ability to deliver innovative and economical products which consistently satisfy the customer. A number of European car manufacturers have some difficulties in both areas, especially in comparison with Japanese producers. These problems must be resolved so that import restrictions can be entirely lifted as planned before the year 2000.

EUROPEAN CAR MANUFACTURERS MUST RECOVER LOST TERRITORY

The market potential of the European car industry shrank considerably during the 1980s. Global presence has continuously decreased. VW, the largest European seller, for example, only has one factory in North America – in Mexico. The factory in Westmoreland was closed in 1990 after continuous losses. VW is hardly represented in Asia, one of the largest expanding markets in the world. They only build the Santana, a German-Chinese co-production, in Shanghai. This is more of a development project, however, than a key to the Asian market of the future. Fiat, Peugeot and Renault also sell almost exclusively on the European market. Even here, they are dependent on their domestic markets for more than 50 per cent of their sales. Our experience shows, however, that a market cannot be held with exports alone. The VW share of the American market, for example, has decreased from 7 per cent (1970) to approximately 1.5 per cent (currently). The Japanese car industry, however, has increasingly changed to manufacturing directly in the foreign markets.

Eight of the nine Japanese car manufacturers are already represented in North America with their own 'transplants' or joint ventures. When they are at full capacity, the Japanese factories in North America will have a production capacity of 2.5 million cars by 1992. By the end of the decade it will also be possible to manufacture over 2 million Japanese cars in Europe. All this indicates that the European car industry must also become a 'global player' in order to be able to respond more directly to the market and be more independent of market conditions. The entire world cannot be supplied with a single model. The dream of an economical 'world car' should have disappeared by now. The global market strategy does require global corporate strategies, but the strategies must vary regionally. The negative effects of the neglected foreign markets are most noticeable during an economic slump in the domestic markets. The home territory in France or Italy, for example, is simply not large enough to effectively balance out variations within the domestic economy.

Entirely new perspectives have emerged for European car manufacturers with the opening up of central and eastern Europe. Sales development is difficult to predict, however, because it greatly depends on the speed of economic development in the former communist countries. Without doubt, the potential is great. In what was formerly West Germany, there are 475 cars to every 1,000 inhabitants. In other words, nearly every other West German has a car. In comparison, there are (per 1,000 inhabitants):

225 cars in eastern Germany,
175 cars in the CSFR,
157 cars in Hungary
127 cars in Bulgaria,
112 cars in Poland,
 56 cars in the CIS, and only
 37 cars in Romania.

The western European car manufacturers have a definite advantage over Japan due to their cultural and geographical proximity to eastern Europe. The Europeans must use this advantage by making direct investments in eastern Europe early in the game. VW has sent an important signal with their investment in Skoda. It will not be long, however, before the Japanese make a move. The markets in central and eastern Europe will not simply be given to the European manufacturers. They, too, must be won against stiff Japanese competition. There are no longer any markets in the world which 'belong' to a country. Each customer wants to be personally convinced and only cars which are better and more economical than the others are convincing. The origin hardly matters any more, especially on the hotly contested foreign markets. A Swiss or Belgian customer does not care if he buys a German or a Japanese car. As almost all large manufacturers export more cars than they sell in their own market, the success of a model is determined by especially critical customers in the 'neutral' markets. Not even the support of the government can change that.

The developments in the American car market show that international joint ventures and cooperation can be advantageous to both sides. The cooperation between the three large American car manufacturers, General Motors, Ford and Chrysler, and Japanese manufacturers has in fact increased considerably. The Americans have an opportunity to study superior Japanese production and management methods and the Japanese profit from the American partners' inside knowledge of the domestic market. This broad-based cooperation also soothes the arguments over trade policy between the two countries. In France or in Germany such joint ventures are still viewed with great scepticism because they are considered a step towards international cartels or go against national pride. However, resisting strategic alliances for ideological reasons is not wise in the long run. Such alliances are often the only feasible way of delivering to previously neglected markets and, thereby, of regaining lost market potential.

PRODUCTIVITY AS THE DECISIVE FACTOR

The key to regaining international competitive ability lies in productivity. The protected manufacturers have the lowest productivity which once again proves that protectionism does not actually protect. Some European manufacturers, however, have not given up demanding protection beyond the self-limitation already agreed to. We should make it clear to these protectionist executives that quotas are always a sign of weakness. It would be extremely foolish for Europeans to give themselves a 'loser image' by placing such demands. The European car industry cannot afford to give the customer the impression that it is completely helpless against the Japanese challenge. Customers want performance. If the European manufacturers want to succeed in the world market, they must begin in their own front yard. It is much harder to convince foreign customers if you cannot even convince your own customers.

In fact, restricting Japanese exports would have provided European manufacturers with little protection. The Japanese are already well established in the Community, as are the American manufacturers Ford and General Motors. There is no longer any doubt that Japanese cars made in the United Kingdom are to be legally considered 'Made in Europe'. This was finally decided by the famous Nissan case. A 'European fortress' could not have been effectively defended against these Japanese transplants. Japanese cars made in the US could also hardly be sent back without starting a trade war between the EC and the US (even though the US does not exactly set a good example by refusing to include the Japanese cars made in Canada in the American-Canadian free trade agreement). This does not, of course, alter the fact that fortresses cannot be defended in modern times. Not one additional European car would be sold in third markets as a result. More likely, even less would be sold because nobody wants to buy from a loser.

THE JAPANESE ADVANTAGE IN PRODUCTIVITY

The overall productivity of European manufacturers is still too low in comparison with that of the Japanese competition. Productivity comparisons conducted by the Massachusetts Institute of Technology (MIT) showed that mass production in a Japanese factory requires an average of 17 working hours to build a car and in a European factory an average of 35 hours. The productivity differential is even larger for luxury cars. The Japanese still require an average of 17 hours per car whereas the European average is 57 hours. This means it takes a Japanese manufacturer, on average, one fourth of the time it takes a European company to manufacture comparable products. If this advantage in production is not eliminated soon it will eventually lead to loss of market shares in higher price classes as well.

The argument often cited by European managers, that the competitive advantage of the Japanese is largely a result of unfair factors, for example in terms of wages or vacation time granted, has been disproved. The Japanese have shown that they can produce more efficiently all over the world and under local conditions (wages and social benefits) than the European car companies. Workers in Japanese factories do not work longer than their European colleagues and still more cars roll off the lines. This 'Japanese miracle' is also happening in the Japanese transplants which is the best proof that it's not a miracle at all. In British factories, for example, Nissan will produce 120,000 cars of the Primera model this year. The added valuation created in Europe is 80 per cent. This example makes it clear that the reasons for higher Japanese productivity must go beyond poor wages or social exploitation.

... through the 'lean production' principle

Many experts consider 'lean production', which is designed to remove obstacles in the entire production process starting with the first supplier and ending with the manufacturer of the final product, to be an important factor of the Japanese productivity advantage. The modern production process employs teams of broadly educated, extremely flexible workers at all levels and an increasing number of automatic machines. This combines the benefits of manual and mass production without the high cost of the former or the inflexibility of the latter. An extra advantage is the capacity to change models more often or deliver to specialized markets, for example off-road vehicles. Traditional production methods are burdened with relatively high costs when manufacturing small lines. The new processes required to produce a different model create a long adjustment period because the process must be completely rearranged. 'Lean production' is better equipped to deal with these problems because production is less rigidly organized and can therefore be constantly developed.

The success of the system depends largely upon the quality of the team. It requires an excellent education and flexibility as well as motivation for solving problems and continuing development. Successful Japanese manufacturers combine high levels of automation with 'lean production'. Automated production is 24 per cent higher than in American companies and 16 per cent more than in European companies. Automation is especially well developed in Japan where the technology is relatively simple and economical. In western factories, however, it is used for more complex tasks which require substantial investments in expensive and specialized equipment. These investments can only be amortized with a correspondingly large level of production. Accordingly, the willingness to change models more frequently is lower, a fact which displeases an increasing number of customers.

... through the 'just-in-time' principle

The successful productivity of Japanese manufacturers is mainly the result of continuous investments in modern technology. The subcontractors are another important factor. Ability and willingness to cooperate play an important role here. Efforts to use the rationalization reserves in non-productive areas more effectively have produced the 'just-in-time' concept. This concept is mainly designed to reduce the manufacturers' warehouse stock and thereby enable a cost saving synchronization of delivery and production. In past years, American and European manufacturers have tried to reduce the Japanese productivity advantage by introducing 'just-in-time' delivery systems. There are, however, still considerable differences between the European and Japanese ideas of 'just-in-time' delivery.

In Europe, 'just-in-time' delivery is often interpreted as simply relocating from the warehouse to the streets, which only relocates the costs instead of actually reducing them. This is especially true when the suppliers are more often 'just in a traffic jam' than they are 'just in time'. New studies show that European subcontractors have great difficulty producing the right amount at the right time. Genuine synchronous production between suppliers and car manufacturers is the exception in Europe. For the most part, the supplier simply creates stores which are then delivered on a 'just-in-time' basis. The real problem is combining this efficient form of warehousing with flexible production methods, ie producing each part at the exact moment it is needed. The Japanese are apparently more successful at this than the Europeans. For this reason, they are not only ahead in serial production methods but are also better able to take individual wishes into account. Japanese car manufacturers often offer packages containing extras which the European manufacturers sell as expensive special wishes. When special wishes are repeatedly asked for, Japanese manufacturers include them in the standard series. We could learn much from the Japanese in this respect as well.

In Japan, parts are delivered as directly to the lines as possible and intermediate storage is avoided. The advantage the Japanese have can be traced directly to the subcontracting structure. Subcontracting is vertically integrated in Japan, ie, a contractor has various subcontractors who mainly deliver to the one contractor. The Japanese manufacturers' tradition of concentrating on a small number of subcontractors has been developed to a strategic advantage. A few selected subcontractors who prove they can meet the highest expectations of quality are bound in lasting relationships. They are included in the development of new car models from the beginning and are, therefore, better able to implement new concepts within 'just-in-time' production.

In Europe, however, a horizontal subcontracting structure has developed. As a result, European car manufacturers, despite manufacturing more of the parts themselves, are supplied by 800 to 2,000 direct subcontractors whereas the Japanese are supplied by 160 to 300. The European suppliers, therefore, do not have a particularly close relationship to the contractor. They are less involved in the technical development of individual parts and their specialized knowledge remains largely unused. The 'co-maker' relationship between car manufacturers and subcontractors common in Japan is not widespread in Europe. This is, in part, due to the greater share of parts which are produced directly by the European manufacturers. There is still too much dependence on in-house research and development instead of creating confidential relationships with the subcontractors. The cheapest subcontractor is seldom also the best. Planning in European companies is obviously more short-term and thus more short-sighted than in Japan, where competitors know exactly when quality or the price is more important.

ONLY ECOLOGICAL CARS HAVE A FUTURE

It is also short-sighted to demand that industrial policy does not further reduce the competitive ability of European car manufacturers with respect to the Japanese by imposing high ecological standards. Nobody can afford to minimize the ecological problems posed by cars. It cannot be denied that cars produce a large part of environmentally damaging emissions. As a result, there is only one solution to the environmental problems: the ecological car. Modern corporate strategy cannot merely use environmental protection as an advertising slogan designed to placate environmental consciousness. Rather, practical steps are needed to reduce pollutants and increase the recycling value of used cars.

The age of the motorcar is not over by any means and we must try to keep it that way, however seemingly 'impossible'. The planned Swatch car with a hybrid engine, electric in city traffic and diesel when needed, is a good idea for cars of the future. We already expect that combustion engines will one day be banned from city centres and large urban areas. If we do not want to be caught sleeping, we must plan for this possibility now. When it is proved that an ecological car is possible, local politicians and environmental protectionists will quickly follow suit, and the second company to offer an ecological car may already be too late.

For these reasons, critical and reliable environmental requirements are an important part of EC industrial policy in the motor sector. This is not a matter of subventions for individual suppliers. Possible solutions must be found on a broad base. The challenges of the future that are related to cars, such as increased energy needs, increased air pollution, acid rain or the greenhouse effect, can only be solved by working together. The research and development policy of the Community can make an important contribution in this area. Between 3 and 7 per cent of annual turnover in the European car industry is invested in research and technology. Almost 65,000 workers are employed in research and development. Europe is at no disadvantage here in comparison with the Japanese who invest approximately 4 per cent of turnover in research and development and employ about 47,000 workers in this area. The broader percentage range in Europe, however, shows that the companies apparently place a varying amount of emphasis on research.

Within the structure of existing research programmes, there are a number of reasons to intensify research activity ranging from design research to production methods. The Europeans still have a clear competitive advantage, at least with regard to European customer tastes. The 'classical lines' are almost exclusively developed in European design studios. However, even this advantage must be continuously defended. Successful designs are much easier to copy than are entire production systems. Another key point of research is car recycling. Car wrecks no longer belong on scrap heaps. They must be recycled as much as possible. This produces interesting future perspectives for other branches of industry, for example, for the steel industry. The development of new production technology is an additional contribution to the strengthening of the European car industry because it would help remove a substantial weakness – the low productivity – while improving quality. Finally, we must consider how the increased use of electronics and control technology can help optimize the driving performance of cars. The future belongs without doubt to the quiet and energy-saving 'clean car'. The age of more horsepower, extremely large spoilers or unnecessary headlights, already being mocked at, is gone forever. More emphasis is being placed on safety and driving comfort. Speed is being replaced by comfort. This opens a number of new development possibilities.

The goal of industrial policy must be to improve the technological basis for the production of ecological and safe cars. Industrial and environmental policies agree completely on this point. High environmental standards correspond with the focal points of research. Complementary to this, favourable conditions must be created for future investments by developing an integrated traffic system and a European traffic infrastructure. Alternative traffic methods, which make restrictions of individual traffic unnecessary, are preferable. Car and rail must no longer be viewed as enemies but must be combined to form a successful team. This will remain an empty slogan until an industrial policy is finally practised which combines ambitious goals of public infrastructure with new technological solutions in a manner which sets a good example to others. There is no doubt that the traffic sector demands new and innovative solutions. Unfortunately, the courage to make investments in trail-blazing 'megaprojects' which also produce technological advancement, is often lacking. Not only road construction is blocked by protests. Fast-train lines and loading terminals for combined traffic, both of which are supposed to provide relief for the roads, also make no headway. The car often remains the only alternative.

WILL THERE BE A RENAISSANCE OF SKILLED LABOUR?

Another important aspect of industrial policy which would increase the strength of the European car industry is training and continuing education. Human capital is extremely important, especially in an area which is as highly technical as the car industry. The new flexible production methods, combined with a high degree of automation, require well-trained workers who are capable of independently solving complicated technical problems. Well-qualified workers are not hard to find, at least not in the German market. An estimated 40 per cent of the employees are skilled labourers, but only 15 per cent use these skills in their jobs. There is a substantial potential of qualifications which is in danger of being lost because the European car industry insists on using the traditional method of mass production, which is characterized by a few easy-to-learn steps. Car workers need only learn simple, manual tasks within mass production systems. The development of production processes in the direction of flexible production requires entirely different skills, however, which must first be 're-learned'. Even the most modern machines are not much good if nobody knows how to operate them.

Establishing an educational network throughout the EC which connects colleges, companies and research centres can contribute to the skilled labourers' mobility and variability within Europe. This is an important prerequisite for the success of new, global strategies, especially regarding joint ventures with international partners. A modern training centre is included in the joint venture being planned in Portugal by VW and Ford for a good reason. Such accompanying measures are necessary if such ambitious projects are to succeed in remote areas.

THE EUROPEAN CAR INDUSTRY IS NOT A SICK PATIENT

During the discussion concerning the competitive ability of European car manufacturers, we may occasionally get the impression that the Europeans are hopelessly inferior to the Japanese in all aspects. It is often forgotten that the EC is still the largest car manufacturer in the world and this branch of industry still operates in the black. The Europeans are still in first place with a world market share of 35 per cent, followed by the US and Japan with 25 per cent each. The car industry is definitely not in a critical condition. We have no reason to complain. On the other hand, we cannot ignore the fact that the growth rate is based chiefly on increased domestic demand. The Europeans have lost ground to the

Japanese in foreign markets, especially in the small- and mid-sized categories. The European car manufacturers must improve their competitive ability over a broad range if they do not want to be beaten in the domestic market as well when the single market is established and the market is opened.

We would be better off accepting the challenge presented by the Japanese than we are by constantly discussing our own weaknesses. This also includes the ability to learn from the Japanese and others. Increasing global presence and improving productivity clearly must be given top priority. There are indications that at least some car manufacturing companies have recognized this fact and are willing to try new methods in both areas. European manufacturers should keep in mind the saying of a Japanese manufacturer: 'Nothing is impossible!'

7

Bundling European Interests: The Shipbuilding Industry

1992 is historic in two respects. First, it will see the completion of the European single market which, at least economically, will overcome the centuries-old splintering of Europe, if at first only among the EC member countries. Second, it is the 500th anniversary of Christopher Columbus's discovery of America. This reminds one of the great maritime tradition which has always been associated with the European continent. Even today, shipbuilding has a great significance for Europe. The EC is the largest trading partner in the world with 90 per cent of the Community's foreign trade taking place by sea. Transportation safety does not require that our exports be transported in European ships, but it is undoubtedly important that our special maritime know-how be maintained in the future.

Short-term economic thinking underestimates the consequences of the downfall of individual industries. Docks cannot be closed and re-opened at the twinkling of an eye depending on the world market situation. Shut-down capacity means the loss not only of jobs but primarily of industrial competence. It is therefore necessary to carefully determine which jobs continue to be profitable under changed conditions and which do not. This is a question of industrial policy in which shipbuilding must be considered. In this connection, account must be taken of the situation of those shipyards which now have to try to offset the loss of military contracts with increasingly civil activities. The special technical know-how of these shipyards could be employed for civil purposes, for example for research and exploitation of the oceans or the development of new unmanned diving vehicles and underwater robots; this presupposes, however, that the shipbuilding industry survives the difficult transitional phase.

RUINOUS INTERNATIONAL COMPETITION

The European maritime industry is subject to extremely ruinous international competition which is not always conducted fairly. It is characterized by an unfair subsidy race. This must be stopped. Although production (delivery) statistics for the years 1986 to 1990 show steadily growing world market shares for the European manufacturers, the trend for new orders is on the decline, not least due to strongly subsidized competition. Although the EC share in 1988 was just under 25 per cent, European shipbuilding participated in slightly under 20 per cent of new orders worldwide in 1990.

Japanese manufacturers in particular press determinedly into the traditional European market segments for high-quality ships. The Japanese government invests the equivalent of over DM 500 million annually in research and development programmes for oceanic and shipbuilding technology in order to develop not only a very fast, technically-advanced supership, but also particularly dependable ship propulsion systems. Moreover, after a 10-year absence from the world market, the US is making a concerted effort to return to commercial shipbuilding. In the light of decreasing military budgets, various manufacturers of warships are also attempting to engage in new activities. The competition is increasing from all sides, and the play is not always fair.

... REQUIRES AN END TO THE SUBSIDY RACE

The first industrial-political task is to stop the subsidy race for shipbuilding, not only in the EC but particularly also worldwide. This is closely tied to the idea of the single market: the economic advantages of the single market can be completely realized only if competition is consistently emphasized as the supporting principle. Here, a strict subsidy control in the EC, and in a countermove the elimination of subsidies in other countries, is required. But even with subsidy elimination there are important gradations. The most negative are operating cost subsidies for truly unprofitable capacity. Since there is no incentive to modernize, these subsidies are a 'bottomless pit'. Somewhat more positive are grants for modernization of shipyards (coupled with the condition of reducing capacity) as well as financial support for new materials within the scope of existing research programmes. A reduction of overcapacity has a price-stabilizing effect for all competitors, and for truly innovative ships no competitor would be disadvantaged. The most unproblematic subsidy is that for creating replacement jobs and associated training. These are actually not subsidies at all, since they eliminate location weaknesses rather than distort competition. As such they can be considered more as investments in the future.

The primary objective, therefore, is to reduce the competition-distorting subsidies in shipbuilding. Although expensive, they rarely increase competitiveness because they freeze aging structures and therefore impede rather than promote structural change. In this respect, all manufacturing countries must pull together so that fair competition can develop. But elimination of subsidies in itself is not sufficient to offer the European shipyards a clear future. An aggravating factor is that shipbuilding is closely linked with other maritime issues related to, for example, ocean resources, ocean pollution or international standards, so that proposals for a sectoral solution offer little help. Up until now there has not been a total European concept for the various maritime challenges, and this presents industrial policy with a separate task.

A COHERENT MARITIME CONCEPT IS NECESSARY

The lack of association between shipbuilding and maritime policy issues represents a significant disadvantage in comparison with countries such as Japan, South Korea or the United States. In Japan, for example, there are close relationships between the maritime trades and shipbuilding, primarily because both operate under the same roof. As a result of its traditional dependence on imports of raw materials and exports of investment goods, Japan has always attached great significance to shipbuilding and maritime commerce. Industry, commerce and transportation often form a tight logical chain, so that each can adapt to the others with maximum effect. This is also true not only for shipbuilding but for ship financing and marketing as well.

These relationships are most evident in the 'home credit scheme', in which Japanese shippers are offered low-cost financing for use primarily to acquire Japanese-built ships. There are similar concerted practices in South Korea. In the course of industrialization based on an export-oriented economy in the 1970s, South Korea established its own shipbuilding and maritime trade industries, although at that time there was overcapacity worldwide. This alone shows the importance which our competitors attach to an efficient maritime trade. But it also makes clear how difficult it is today to assert oneself in the world market. When two large shipbuilding nations, which are also large trading countries, create their own domestic market which is practically immune to the outside, then this is a significant competitive disadvantage for the remaining shipbuilding countries. The overcapacity has an even more powerful effect on the remaining markets.

THREE IMPORTANT REASONS FOR A COMMUNITY INITIATIVE

Nevertheless, the need for an independent European shipbuilding industry is not acknowledged by everyone. According to one popular line of reasoning, one could buy ships where the prices are most favourable. The departure of European shipbuilders from the market is no different from the competitive survival processes in other economic areas. But this is economically and politically too short-sighted. There is a whole series of reasons for retaining one's own, efficient shipbuilding industry. First, the Community needs a dependable, efficient EC fleet, not only as a trading nation but also for internal commerce. Approximately one-third of the domestic trade in the EC is carried out by ocean and inland shipping. After selection of the most important competitors, the subsidy race would be replaced by the price dictation of a narrow oligopoly. The EC therefore has a basic interest in retaining competitive market structures in order to avoid becoming unilaterally dependent.

Secondly, shipbuilding today is the result of the combined effects of several factors. Maritime research, shippers, shipyards, suppliers and outfitters form a closely-knit relationship, which together determines competitiveness. A loss of industrial competence would at the same time destroy these networks and bring all the disadvantageous consequences for jobs in the subordinate sectors. It is not at all a question of unskilled jobs, which would fall victim to rationalization in any case, but rather of highly qualified engineering consultants and specialized suppliers, whose know-how can be useful for other industrial areas also.

Maritime activities are becoming technically more demanding. A modern cruise ship has as much electronic equipment as many warships or the cockpit of a jet aeroplane. The EC cannot survive economically either as a 'blueprint company' or as a pure consumer society. We also need to retain our industrial skills. In this respect, shipbuilding is a key branch because it demands a combination of exacting technical knowledge and trade skills. A lot of welding will be required in the future but it must be more precise and use higher-quality materials. We therefore must not put our great maritime expertise to one side but rather continue to develop it according to our objectives.

A third reason for a European shipbuilding policy is that the significance of shipbuilding extends far beyond its own sector. The oceans form an increasingly important aspect of life for the human race. They contain important resources such as food, fossil energy reserves, minerals and biotopes. Advances in maritime research offer new perspectives for their application. For example, technological processes allow the extraction of minerals from very great depths. Growing along with a consciousness of the importance of sea resources is also concern for the increasing pollution of the oceans. Serious tanker accidents, for example off Alaska and in the Mediterranean, underline the need for stricter international regulation and safety measures. If the Europeans want to participate here, they must continue to build their own ships, in order to gather experience and – when needed – to bring about stricter standards internationally. We need tankers which do not break apart so easily and methods of exploration which protect the environment. Some things can be achieved through stricter regulations, others only through increased research and new techniques. The Community must play a leading role in both cases.

The maritime future of the Community depends on the competitiveness of its maritime industries. Only efficient maritime industries can guarantee that the EC continues to hold a position from which it can participate in world trade and exploit the oceans reasonably and successfully. The resulting maritime technology industry possesses a great potential. Experts estimate the world market volume in this area today at DM 50 billion a year. In the light of the heavy pollution however, additional investments in the safety of off-shore drilling rigs and platforms are unavoidable. The EC desperately needs its own 'standing' in order to push through its high safety standards; otherwise, it must accept the lower safety standards of other nations. The 'ship of the future' cannot be invented by politicians, only by shipbuilders and shipyards. It would be a setback if the EC was to return to the old sectoral industrial policy and make a point of promoting selected maritime projects. Having set an initiative and completed a catch-up phase, even Japanese industrial policy has moved toward broad support of cross-sectional technologies: there is no selective, project-oriented assistance any longer.

A HORIZONTAL CONCEPT FOR SHIPBUILDING

The EC can be active only peripherally in solving maritime problems. An initial industrial policy starting point for the support of shipbuilding is therefore, as so often, an emphasis on research and development. The EC world market share in shipbuilding is based primarily on the production of specialized ships. In this way European manufacturers continue to enjoy a certain competitive advantage despite higher costs. For some time, however, the Japanese have been getting a foothold in this market segment with increasing success.

... through common research

The Japanese challenge presents the Europeans with very serious problems. The Europeans work in an extremely splintered market and show little interest in closer cooperation, especially in the research area. The potential for new shipbuilding technologies, for example with respect to new off-shore structures, surface propulsion or deep-sea mining equipment, is thus of limited use. A coordinated concept at the Community level is urgently needed. Customers, manufacturers and suppliers must exchange their expertise and adapt to each other, so that reasonable focal points for European research programmes can be defined. However, the research programmes must lead to workable designs that are subject to demand. It is important, therefore, that where appropriate manufacturers and users be involved in the research programmes.

... through the elimination of technical barriers

A further maritime focal point lies in the elimination of technical barriers, ie, in improving the business environment. The European industry for marine outfitting comprises predominantly medium sized enterprises which are not active solely in the maritime area. There is in Europe no specialized marine outfitting industry. In contrast, Japanese and South Korean outfitters form a highly specialized industry and are able, because of their higher turnover, to offer more favourable conditions than their significantly smaller European competitors. Through the realization of the EC single market and the elimination of technical trade barriers, better conditions are being developed in the Community for an internationally competitive outfitting industry. The Commission is working on a guideline which will harmonize the technical regulations of a marine outfitting industry. This guideline is intended to address safety aspects as well as the technical measures for preventing pollution of the oceans by dangerous substances. Generally applicable standards would enable the production of outfitting equipment for the entire single market. This would be an important step toward an internationally competitive supply industry for marine outfitting.

... through coordinated international appearances

Although the EC is on the way to political union, the practical realization of its interests is exceedingly sluggish. The Community's international bodies for maritime commerce and shipbuilding still do not speak with one voice. The Commission has only an observer status in the maritime bodies which deal with the technical and social issues of maritime commerce. Unlike the other maritime nations, such as the US, Japan or the former Soviet Union, all of which represent their interests energetically, the EC countries often cannot achieve a common position. This impedes considerably the realization of European interests in the maritime area.

The international bodies by no means control only technical details. Often, concrete economic or scientific interests are behind supposedly 'technical' decisions. For example, in 1990 the US established unilateral regulations whereby new tankers entering US ports had to possess double hulls. On the other hand, the Japanese are suggesting as an alternative the between-deck tanker developed by a leading Japanese shipyard. The Europeans will have to agree on a unified position or be forced to accept that of the others. Through the splintering of European interests, the member countries deprive themselves of the chance to exert a lasting influence on important maritime-political issues. A more effective representation of interests by the Commission or at least by a genuine coordination of the member countries is therefore also an important element of maritime EC industrial policy.

... through a bundling of maritime interests

Unlike other sectors, an efficient maritime policy depends upon a close cooperation between the various member countries, research institutes, universities and the European Commission. Maritime know-how is extremely complex and often the result of centuries-old maritime tradition. Both business and government must look for ways to bring the different decision-makers together at one table to better coordinate their actions. It is this framework which permits discussion of overlapping interests, such as standards, research programmes, port facilities or environmental questions, and thus enables the development of common projects and strategies. I support a discussion forum in which shipyards, marine outfitters, port authorities, safety experts, maritime research institutes and the economic authorities of the member countries are represented.

The 'ship of the future' cannot be developed in a dry dock. It must, possibly with public funding, be scientifically researched, properly engineered and professionally built in a shipyard, possibly as a demonstration project. To permit it to operate in European waters, it needs an official type approval, and the ports may require additional precautions. If other countries are to assume the standards thereby developed and implemented in practice, the EC must 'sell' the project to the international bodies. Only when this all fits together will the world be open to European shipbuilding. Many must work towards the same goal together if it is to be a success. The shipyards cannot accomplish such a breakthrough on their own.

One can imagine the accusations against such an integrated concept. Such a bundling together of maritime interests will be seen as a monopoly and inconsistent with a market economy. This would be a crude misinterpretation, however, since the task of the forum should be limited to identifying the most important areas in which common European interests prevail and where (safeguarding the subsidiary principle) measures at the EC level would be appropriate. In this way, standards could be developed, research priorities determined or trendsetting infrastructure projects thought out. There is absolutely no reason to avoid this contact with each other. There is no dearth of maritime issues which can be resolved only in close cooperation: What effect do global transport systems have on the shipyards? What do freight carriers expect from the shipping and port authorities? How can the technology transfer between military and civilian areas be improved? What new developments are there for exploiting ocean resources? What tanker size should be permitted for which waters? What recommendations are there for international standards? Who should present them and push them through? There is, therefore, sufficient material for common discussion, but there is unfortunately no suitable forum. The creation of such a maritime forum is truly a European concern.

CREATING CLUSTERS

Behind this idea stands the conviction that efficient institutions are at least as decisive for market success as efficient markets. It is always the combined effect of both factors that determines the quality of the location. Markets tend toward short-term thinking, and this is no less true for politicians. It is the combination of both which promises the greatest success. Successful industries are for the most part closely 'internetted' with other industries, but also with governmental research facilities, standards institutes or systems for professional development or quality assurance. We must also create these 'clusters' to a greater degree for European shipping. The European shipyard industry can assert itself in fair competition only if sufficiently large productivity and innovational advances can be achieved. Innovations are not developed in secret session but rather are based on efficient interaction between government, business and science. It is therefore primarily a question of creating efficient structures for this complex coordination process.

Of course, in a market economy the enterprises must bear the responsibility of planning, and the risk of a failure must not be underwritten by the government. But the prerequisite for the individual planning horizon can be improved if more transparency prevails concerning what the other is planning. Ships need ports and ports depend on the efficiency of trans-shipment terminals and inland transportation. Each forms only a small link in this transportation chain and therefore cannot exert much influence on public decisions. Only through cooperation and sharing of information can a well-rounded maritime concept for Europe arise from this disconnected coexistence of the individual links.

8

More European Cooperation: The Aviation Industry

The international market for aircraft is a growth market, but it is more than that. Aircraft have always drawn political attention; partly for military reasons, and partly because aviation and space travel were long considered the industry of the future, bar none. Even if both of these factors do not have as convincing an effect as a few years ago, the aviation industry remains strongly dependent on political direction. What role can the European industrial policy play in this case?

FAVOURABLE GROWTH PERSPECTIVES FOR EUROPEAN AIRCRAFT

The primary factor for future growth perspectives in the European aviation industry is the demand for aircraft, which in turn depends on the growth of aviation. Aviation has grown strongly within the last 30 years: from 1975 to the present, it tripled and experts estimate that by the year 2000, it will double again. Seen as a whole therefore, the aviation industry is a growth industry, which can continue to expect strong growth rates. But the rosy outlook for the future is clouded again and again by strong economic fluctuations. For example, after the oil crisis of 1979 total demand dropped considerably, and the latest Gulf crisis has also left its traces in the manufacturers' order books. Orders were cancelled or delayed because each economic crisis rapidly subjects the airline industry to liquidity bottle-necks. Although the aircraft market is really a seller's market (because more aircraft are demanded than can ever be built), there are always short-term demand fluctuations which require staying power and considerable financial reserves from the manufacturers. The peculiarities of the production process make it extremely difficult to react to such economic developments in the short term.

... BUT SOME RISK FACTORS

The big sellers are presently aircraft with seating capacities exceeding 100. The manufacturers of these aircraft have full order books; production is booked through to 1995 and beyond. The further market forecasts are also extremely favourable. Experts estimate that the growth of the civil aviation industry could, in the long term, lie significantly above the industrial average. But unexpected setbacks which are impossible to predict can certainly occur. Airspace cannot be expanded as desired. The 'holding patterns' over the large airports are becoming increasingly longer. Departure delays are so frequent that for short distances it does not pay to book a flight. The train or motorcar is often significantly faster, especially when one considers the long drive to the airport and the long waiting times.

Another risk factor is that several large airlines are already in the red. In the US, deregulation led to a drastic increase in competition with passengers benefitting from lower fares. But deregulation has now triggered a consolidation in the American airlines, with the result that flights have been cut back and fares are again on the increase. The growing significance of leasing companies, which lease aircraft to different airlines, changes the demand situation: first, because at order time the aircraft manufacturers do not negotiate with the actual operator; and second, because the fleet is utilized more efficiently. Due to their relatively thin capitalization the leasing firms cannot be considered secure customers, so that the manufacturers' risk of loss increases because orders are cancelled frequently and often at short notice.

The high and increasing market risks in the aircraft business have up till now been cushioned by new market outlets, for example in Asia and the Pacific, as well as by the accelerated replacement of older aircraft. The world market share for civil jet aircraft of European origin is currently approximately 30 per cent; the large remainder is covered by American manufacturers, which thereby enjoy an undisputed, market dominating position. For the smaller aircraft – for example, aircraft for regional routes, business aircraft, lightweight aircraft or commercial helicopters – which make up roughly 20 per cent of the total turnover, the Europeans play a more significant role. European manufacturers have about three-quarters of the world market for regional aircraft, a third of the world market for business and lightweight aircraft, and slightly over a third of the world market for commercial helicopters. In the course of the last 15 years, the Europeans have been able to register good sales success, even in the American market. Between 1975 and 1991 their market share in the US rose from 1 per cent to almost 30 per cent (the Airbus played a significant role).

RE-CONVERSION AS A NEW CHALLENGE

In the light of dwindling military demand, the significance of the civil sector will increase in the coming years. For many enterprises the opportunities to compensate losses on the civil side with gains from military demand no longer exists. In the past American manufacturers in particular had made excellent use of these chances for cross-subsidizing from the military to the civil areas. The elimination of this particular form of subsidy will contribute to equal opportunities in competition but, at the same time the subsidies for the European aircraft industry will come increasingly under critical fire.

For this reason, structural changes are unavoidable for outfitters, component manufacturers and subcontractors. Enterprises which up till now were suppliers or even system manufacturers in the military area will attempt more and more to establish a footing as suppliers or subcontractors in the civil area. This will lead to increased competitive pressure at the supplier level. Approximately half of current production in the European aviation industry applies to military equipment, primarily fighter aircraft, helicopters and missiles. Despite weak growth rates in the military budgets in recent years, the production of military equipment has even increased. The Europeans have succeeded in fulfilling more military contracts from their own production. Furthermore, demand from third-party countries for military aircraft from the Community has increased sharply. Fortunately, however, military production in Europe is no longer the deciding factor for growth in the aviation industry, even though present capacity is still high. The special problem lies in the strong geographical concentration of the military production locations. The extent to which the conversion from military to civil aircraft can be eased by industrial policy must be examined, so that the highly skilled jobs in this branch can remain and regional imbalances avoided.

THE EUROPEAN AVIATION INDUSTRY MUST UNDERGO RESTRUCTURING

The generally positive starting position cannot disguise the fact that the Europeans have significant competitive structural disadvantages compared to their main American competitors. It would therefore be wrong to trust too much in the high growth rates of recent years, because there is too much going on. The favourable updrafts for the branch can quickly reverse, and it will then be a question of whether the European manufacturers' resources can withstand a long period of 'drought'. Here, one has to visualize that the market for aircraft is a strongly concentrated one. The predominant market form is, for technical reasons, an oligopoly of a small number of market leaders. In Europe, the aviation industry is concentrated primarily in four countries: Great Britain (35 per cent), France (30 per cent), Germany (22 per cent), and Italy (8 per cent). The other European manufacturing countries are the Netherlands (3 per cent), Spain (2 per cent), and Belgium (1 per cent). In the past, there has been little large scale international cooperation between the European companies. Aircraft continue to have high national symbolic value, something which considerably impedes cooperation among the European partner countries.

...AIRBUS AS AN EXAMPLE OF EUROPEAN COOPERATION

Up till now the Airbus has been the sole showpiece of European cooperation. Airbus has developed into a manufacturer with worldwide recognition; the aircraft are competitive, of high quality and equipped with the most advanced technology. The founding of Airbus Industries has therefore paid off. At any rate, the Europeans have in this way succeeded in not leaving the oligopolistic market to the Americans. Whoever criticizes the establishment and extension of the Airbus family as a violation of free-market rules overlooks, or wants to overlook, the fact that market-based principles apply only in a limited sense to the market for wide-bodied aircraft. Apart from Airbus Industries there are only two other manufacturers in the world, namely Boeing and McDonnell Douglas. The founding of the Airbus consortium has for this reason led to more competition and reduced the unilateral dependency on the Americans. That should please the anti-trust watchdogs, but many apparently find it difficult to think in these categories of worldwide competition.

... BUT WITH WEAKNESSES

So far 700 Airbus aircraft have been sold and delivered; others are on order. However, the penetrating market success of the Airbus is no reason for self-satisfaction. Although the Airbus is a European aircraft, the thinking and action taken by the individual industries is based primarily on national interests. When Airbus Industries was founded, consideration for national, partly political, interests was necessary. In the light of these initial conditions, the Airbus model performs exceedingly well. And yet it represents a compromise which cannot remain as it is.

The greatest weakness is the lack of entrepreneurial thinking, which is too often impeded by national considerations. Since the partners are at the same time owners and producers, each one attempts to optimize the relationship of production to capital share for itself. Pushed to extremes, as far as bargaining for production shares is concerned, the present model functions according to the 'beggar my neighbour' principle, ie, each attempts to win the largest and most lucrative share of the contracts. In this way the so-called 'industrial lead' becomes a special trophy, since it determines which partner is presented to the public as the aircraft manufacturer. Considering the production and sales figures achieved to this point, this model, which ranks efficiency below vanity, is no longer adequate.

Common European interest is still directed primarily in research and development of new types of aircraft, but when the Airbus family is completed the interest will shift more strongly toward production. At this time, one of the most important reasons for subsidizing the Airbus, namely the underwriting of development risks, will lose significance. At some point, the project must stand on its own two feet, since continuing production subsidies are clear violations of the GATT agreements. What can be done to improve the competitiveness of the Airbus under these conditions? Most observers agree that Airbus Industries itself needs more entrepreneurial authority. A step in this direction would be the reorganization of the holding company as a limited company. This transformation could occur along with a new distribution of authorities as well as new, more efficient decision-making and production structures. In this case, it is not at all important who the owner is. Owners can be private individuals as well as governments. In the necessary structural changes for Airbus, the primary question is not of privatization of the enterprise, even though this certainly would be an advantage. The deciding factor is rather that the enterprise operate on a private (ie, profit-oriented) basis. If governments can summon up this discipline, there are no reservations against government-owned companies. Even the EEC treaty is neutral in this respect.

MAKING LOCATION DECISIONS BASED ON RATIONAL CRITERIA

As far as Airbus is concerned, we are still far removed from political abstinence. The example of the discussion about the location for the final assembly of the A321 proves that national proportionality considerations still override those for economic efficiency. Considering the present division of labour, the German decision for Hamburg may be defensible. But it is questionable whether this would also be the case if one of the goals were economic optimization, independent of quotas. A concentration of final assembly operations at one location might, from an economic vantage point, be several times more efficient than a distribution among different regions in the Community. The necessary investment sums would then undoubtedly be lower and could amortize more rapidly. At the same time, the opportunities would be greater to react flexibly to structural changes in demand. Greater demand fluctuations for the A321 cannot be compensated by switching to final assembly of other aircraft. This could prove to be a painful cost factor if demand unexpectedly fluctuates.

The aviation industry is for many a key industry which must be supported for strategic reasons. The European aviation industry has after all a turnover of approximately DM 75 billion, which amounts to about 3 per cent of total European industrial production. Only in a limited way, however, do these figures say anything about the economic significance of this sector. Aircraft construction is high technology, and this is reflected in the large share of the research and development costs. Approximately 15 per cent of turnover is invested in research and development. In this respect the aviation industry occupies third place after the electronics and chemical industries. It is an undisputed fact that Airbus builds technically outstanding aircraft, but weaknesses still exist in production. To put it clearly: Airbus Industries produces too expensively. Aircraft prices are determined primarily by the world market, where Boeing is the undisputed price setter. Airbus has to orient itself to this fact, but because of the numerous overlaps, additional costs arise which are difficult to recover. The sales successes of Airbus rest on an extremely questionable base.

TECHNOLOGICAL SUPERIORITY IS NOT ENOUGH

One can only speak of Airbus as a true success when it sells as many aircraft as are sold by the competition. With Airbus, European civil aviation is confronted with an extremely difficult question of principle: either Airbus closes ranks with world leader Boeing, or it will be difficult to ever obtain prices that cover costs. Until that time European industry has some catching up to do. Europeans do not have the necessary flexibility to react quickly to a strong increase in demand, nor can the synergism between military and civil activities, as it exists in the US, be exploited in Europe. This interaction serves to keep the utilization of capacity in the US at a constant level. The result: economic stimuli benefit American industry first, because capacity is held there in reserve for military use in times of a recession. This opportunity for compensation is absent in Europe and this is a serious competitive disadvantage.

It is the mass production of the American aircraft industry which makes it possible to reach cost-saving degression effects and thus to make cost-effective bids. The lack of such a savings possibility in Europe strongly limits our industrial competitiveness at present. Only mass production at a constantly high level would enable the high fixed costs of a new programme to be distributed over a large number of aircraft. The same degression effect can be achieved if past experience is used for new programmes. For this reason, it is important to develop well-rounded aircraft families and to derive several models from existing programmes. This not only rounds off the sales programme but it also has a cost-saving effect in production. The concept of a well-rounded product line is in the meantime being implemented by Airbus, but with less effectiveness than in the US. The striving for technical perfection is sometimes more strongly evident than the desire to reduce costs. Here the optimum utilization of the production facilities would be of decisive significance, but it is exactly here that the national interests collide with economic efficiency thinking. When in doubt, those who make the subsidy decisions maintain the upper hand, so that prestige and national pride often count more than entrepreneurially rational decisions.

A HIGH EXCHANGE RATE RISK REMAINS A COMPETITIVE DISADVANTAGE

The high exchange rate risk represents a particular handicap for the European aviation industry. The dollar is still the undisputed reference currency for aircraft trade. The possibility of another currency, for example the ECU, taking over the dollar's role in this area is not foreseeable at the present time. The European aviation industry will have to continue to live with this currency-related competitive disadvantage. It is therefore essential to look for other ways, which are politically and economically defensible, to compensate. Mere subsidies as compensation for the exchange rate risk do not offer much help. The discussion about the exchange rate clause when Daimler Benz took over MBB has repercussions even today. In this debate, the deciding factor is unfortunately drowned out again and again, namely that it was a question of making a contribution over the longer term toward the reduction of subsidies. The participation of private investors is here the best prerequisite. The limited-time exchange rate guarantee of the German federal government was, so to speak, the price for a take-over by private means. This was not disputed by the Americans at the time. In a meeting with then US Trade Representative Clayton Yeutter in London, I, as Federal Economic Minister, received an explicit agreement on subsidies which served to privatize Airbus. Some apparently do not want to remember that today, as this difficult operation was successfully accomplished in the face of considerable resistance.

Despite this, the national governments in Europe are still called upon to cushion the exchange rate risk of the European aviation industry. It is conceivable that, for example, in times of a high dollar exchange rate, tax-free reserves could be maintained. Such reserves, which are affected only by exchange rate policy, could be correspondingly tapped by industry in times of a weak dollar – a concept somewhat analogous to the US strategic oil reserve. This example also shows how important it is to have a strong currency of one's own which can also assume the role of a lead currency. The Deutschmark would be hopelessly overtaxed in this respect. I do not at all understand the concerns which arise, especially from the German side, concerning a unified European currency. As an object of speculation, the Deutschmark endangers not only German exports but carries other currencies along with it as well. What it costs when one is forced to invoice in a foreign currency is shown most clearly in the Airbus case. For reasons of industrial policy as well, we desperately need a European currency which is strong enough to prevail worldwide as a medium of exchange.

IDEAS FOR A EUROPEAN INDUSTRIAL POLICY

At this point, what can European industrial policy do to make a concrete contribution to improving the competitiveness of the European aviation industry? What is true for Airbus, ships or semiconductors must also hold true for aircraft: the main responsibility rests with the economic players themselves. The national governments also remain responsible as long as most of the European enterprises remain government-owned. One should not expect too much of the EC in this respect. The contribution from Brussels can be seen as a supplement. However, the positive echo concerning the position of the Commission toward the aviation industry ('a competitive European aviation industry'), which I delivered to the Council at the beginning of 1991, shows the high level of interest which the industry as well as the member countries have toward a European industrial policy in this important future-oriented sector.

... through international cooperation

The fact that a solution to the aforementioned problems is no longer possible at the national level must now be faced. An international cooperation within the Community has proved to be almost essential for survival. The Community cannot avoid establishing a suitable framework for this. It also holds true that the realization of the single market will facilitate the integration of the European aviation industry. Although the demand for commercial aircraft will remain largely unchanged, the single market will at the same time allow more favourable conditions for a strong coalescence in the European aviation industry. Not only will the climate become thereby more 'European', but European cooperation will be eased by the modified legal environment. That allows the aviation industry to grow into industrial structures which are comparable in size to those of the competition.

There are still differing technical regulations and certification procedures for individual components in the member countries. The competitive disadvantage resulting from this is obvious. For some time, the European association of aviation and space manufacturers (AECMA) has participated actively in the European committee for standardization (CEN) in order to eliminate the technical trade obstacles resulting from different standards. The civil aviation authorities in the individual member countries are responsible for the certification procedure. In this case, it is a question of achieving an optimum safety level while at the same time reducing certification costs. Only then will free trade in aviation products be guaranteed within the Community. Efforts to harmonize certification are being promoted by the national civil aviation authorities in the framework of the Joint Aviation Authorities (JAA). This consolidation extends to countries outside the European Community. The attempt is being made to develop a common safety concept. The Commission supports the activities of the JAA and supports further the creation of a European civil aviation authority. Corresponding work has been started.

... through cooperation in research

Advanced technology in design, engines and in outfitting aircraft are decisive conditions for future commercial success. Through better coordination of research activities on the European level, public funding can be more objective-oriented and subject to less economic leakage. In this way, excess costs can be reduced and technical synergism effects attained. The independent action of enterprises may have had its value in the past because extensive support could be sustained relatively easily. Each member country supported 'its own' companies, in the hope of acquiring contracts for itself. This practice cannot continue in the same manner in the future. The rising system costs, as well as the foreseeable cutbacks in support by the national governments, require a closer cooperation between the players in order to eliminate the inefficiency which is built into the system.

In the research area, the Community is not starting from square one. In March 1989, the Council established the research programme BRITE/EURAM, which includes a two-year pilot programme for research activities in the aviation area. Further Community actions can follow if this initiative proves valuable. The Community can also be a bridge builder in the shift from military to civil production, for example by supporting research work on a new supersonic aeroplane. Such a supersonic aircraft can be realized only in close European cooperation, perhaps only with the Americans and possibly the Japanese. It is also true that salvation for the aviation industry is not necessarily found in 'European champions'.

... through an end to the international subsidy race

The preservation of free and undistorted competition is one of the basic principles of the Community. The international context in which the European aviation industry is active also requires strict adherence to the GATT rules. The Community is interested in a rapid re-negotiation of the GATT code for aircraft. This new framework would render superfluous the argument about which standards must be used for measuring the Airbus subsidies and also those for Boeing and McDonnell Douglas. To put it plainly: the Europeans too are against a subsidy race. The subsidy ban for the production of aircraft is not at issue. The only question is to what extent the public sector can support new research and development programmes in the future. In this respect, European notions lie slightly higher than the American ones, since European manufacturers cannot profit from the synergism effects of military research. But even this small difference of opinion does not change the fact that all direct and indirect subsidies need to be examined.

In the past, the entire aviation industry received significant assistance. It is time to make a clean break with the past. What is necessary now is guaranteeing the transparency of government financing, whatever type it might be. Transparency is the first step in reducing government subsidies. The EC can be an inspector in this area. The competitiveness of the aviation, and other industries, can be strengthened in the short and middle term only without government subsidies. It is therefore in the interest of all parties to progressively cut back public assistance. Of course, the EC cannot do this alone – our most important competitors have to do their share.

... through a European legal framework

The Europeans do not have the same legal structures as their competitors. At the present time, common activities can be undertaken only in the framework of the European economic interest association. This framework is relatively limited, however, since commercial activities are not affected. Europe Ltd, as proposed to the Ministerial Council by the Commission, could create the legal framework enabling an adaptation of industrial and economic structures to the size of the market. The transformation of Airbus Industries into a European limited company would not only be a symbolic step; under the legal form of Europe Ltd, Airbus could prove that the new legal structure also leads to economic optimization of the total model.

... through a European merger control aimed at the world market

The assessment criteria of the merger control regulation passed by the Council in 1989 can also be applied to the aviation area. Here, the economic and industrial peculiarities of the aviation industry must be taken into consideration. No market participant is in a position to provide the high funding required today for aircraft construction. The national markets have become too narrow to enable such development by enterprises in the form of the large European airlines. Whatever companies want to survive in the aviation industry must also have global development opportunities. However, creation of enterprise units at the European level which cover the entire supply capacity in all areas does not lead automatically to the creation or strengthening of dominance in a common market.

Positively stated: whoever wants to be successful at building aircraft today needs a large market share in Europe to be competitive internationally. In this connection the merger injunction against Aerospatiale, Alenia and de Havilland, which together planned to develop 20- to 70-seat regional aircraft, has caused some excitement. The merger of these three firms would have truly led to the situation in which the new enterprise would have a 50 per cent world market share. The argument that Boeing possesses a similar dominating position for jet aircraft is not convincing. Mergers must be judged differently from internal growth, as far as competition is concerned. On the other hand, one can pose the question whether the consortium would have achieved a truly monopoly-like position, since there are in Europe other strong contenders who could also have joined together. It cannot be disputed that the world market is the sole relevant frame of reference. The high development costs, regional aircraft included, do not allow a large number of companies in this market segment to operate competitively. Therefore, a restructuring of the European aviation industry is in any case unavoidable. The planned merger would have been the first step toward a long-term competitive European industry. Now we must wait to see which merger case is decided next. In each case, as for the first merger injunction, industrial–political decisions will be made. Perhaps that will later put this decision in another light, one which is not as bright from a competition point of view.

The example of a 100-seat regional aircraft shows how important European cooperation has become in the meantime. In this market segment, there are only two US manufacturers: Boeing with the 737-500 and McDonnell Douglas with the MD87. The Europeans are competing heavily among each other: British Aerospace is planning a new edition of its 146 aircraft; Fokker intends to develop a stretch version of the current Fokker 100; Alenia, Aerospatiale and DASA, the so-called southern connection, have decided on construction of a common aircraft. It is still uncertain whether Airbus will also engage itself in this market segment by building an A319. A short version of the A320 would certainly be of great interest among airlines desiring to fill out the Airbus family toward the low end. The economic players must decide whether four versions of a European 100-seat regional aircraft are necessary. Doubts are at least in order. From a European standpoint, it would be desirable to concentrate energies in this area, in order to survive internationally. But it may also be true, as others maintain, that the Europeans must build at least two aircraft for this market segment in order to maintain international competition. After all, the Europeans currently have a significant market share in third countries, including the US.

DEPARTURE FROM NATIONAL STRATEGIES

At the Commission's suggestion, the European Council has resolved to intensify the expansion of European networks. An important pillar within the networks is the development of the transportation network, which includes not only the development of corresponding infrastructures, such as airfields, but also the expansion of air transportation. The control of aviation in Europe must be improved. This includes, for example, an equalization of aviation activities, which at the present time are concentrated at a few major airports. The development of a European regional aviation network is welcome not only from a traffic policy perspective. Certain regions in the Community would become more attractive in this way. With that, the locational advantage of decentralization in the Community would increase. Liberalizing European aviation would contribute to this. In the future, the airlines in the EC are to be able to determine take-offs and landings freely within the Community. The regional airports especially will profit greatly from this, because the large aviation centres are already heavily overloaded. This in turn increases the chances for mid-range regional aircraft, in which the Europeans are particularly competitive.

Most industrial and service sectors today are marked by strong international integration. Up till now, the European aviation industry represented the exception to this rule, although the market actually has international dimensions. European industry, the member countries and the EC Commission are attempting in concert to close this gap. The decisive factor is that the member countries distance themselves from purely national strategies. This is still a relic from the time in which the aviation industry was stamped by defence interests.

These times however are gradually passing. A common foreign and security policy in the Community will contribute to overcoming existing reservations. While enterprises bear the main responsibility for the utilization of further synergy effects, it is the Community's responsibility to give the necessary impulse for stronger European cooperation. An initial dialogue between the enterprises, the member countries and the EC Commission has been successfully started. We stand, however, only at the beginning of a process from which Europe hopefully will emerge economically and politically stronger.

9

The Key to the Future: The Electronics Industry

There are few areas which play such a decisive role for future economic development as electronics. At the millennium, the electronics industry will be the most important economic sector of all. Even today, this sector has the highest growth rate. A clear trend is evident from 'hard' to 'soft' – from equipment manufacture toward software. The significance of the electronics industry reaches far beyond its direct share of the gross national product. The common characteristic of the various electronics branches is the 'information' element. Aside from information technology in the narrower sense, this encompasses manufacture, processing and forwarding of information, the basic material of a modern industrial society. In this respect, the electronics industry is not only the drive mechanism but the lubrication as well.

Just as the first industrial revolution depended on coal and steel, present development is driven predominantly by electronics. But unlike the materials in the industrial revolution, electronics permeates all facets of the economy. The difference between high- and low-tech has long since lost its importance. Electronics has become an ever-present raw material without which competitive products or production processes can no longer be manufactured. The industrial future of Europe depends strongly on the availability of this precious resource. That is no overstatement.

IS THE EUROPEAN ELECTRONICS INDUSTRY LOSING TOUCH?

Where exactly does the electronics industry stand in the Community? This question cannot be answered so easily. The European market share in the various branches of electronics varies. In telecommunications and information services the Community does not enjoy a bad position at all. The outlook is different for semiconductors, information technology and peripheral devices. In these areas, the Community threatens to lose touch with the world market competition. In entertainment electronics there are still only two large manufacturers in the EC. Overall therefore, there is a very mixed picture, allowing no clear conclusions as to the competitiveness of the European electronics industry.

What can be ascertained in any case is a relapse of Europe from second to third place in electronics behind the US and Japan. Significant losses are incurred in some electronics branches within Europe. The balance of trade in important sectors also shows strong shifts to the disfavour of the Europeans. Even where sectoral imbalances between production and demand appear to be less pronounced, a closer look reveals clear weaknesses. The European production of video recorders does not at all represent a competitive strength of European industry. European production is rather being fed intravenously by Japanese technology. This is even more true for camcorders, which are not manufactured in the EC at all.

... strong splintering of the European market

There are a series of structural reasons for the relative weaknesses of the European electronics industry. On the demand side, a large uniform market has been missing up till now. The EC markets are much too splintered. This is also a problem in electronics. Mass production advantages and rationalization opportunities can therefore not be optimally utilized. Differing technical standards have an especially disadvantageous effect. Since national standards are oriented predominantly toward the efficiency of one's own industry and not toward the world market, they hold the enterprises to a certain extent hostage in a gilded cage. That is an example of bad industrial policy, even if some firms imagine for themselves a short-term competitive advantage. This is however a miscalculation. Technical standards which deviate from international standards block the national market in both directions: although entry is made more difficult for foreign competitors, the home industry fails to negotiate the leap across the border, because the foreign markets in turn require completely different standards. Only world-class companies are in a position to produce 18 or more different plugs and to abide by a different technical standard for each country. For the smaller European firms, on the other hand, such confusion means certain departure, sooner or later. Many realized that too late. Although the single market came late for them, it is hopefully not too late for others.

... lack of demand for European technology

A further deficiency in the Community is that international user networks have been practically non-existent up till now. Consumers seem to accept technical innovations in Europe less readily than they do in other markets. In some member countries, new technologies are often debated so long that other countries have already gone into mass production with them. In a technology-hostile environment, a competitive electronics industry has difficulty asserting itself. The quality of demand is also a competitiveness factor, and in this respect the American and Japanese manufacturers enjoy a much more experimental public in their domestic markets. The following is true in electronics: each country gets the industry it deserves. Deficiency in competitiveness can also have its origins in missing or unimaginative demand. That is especially true for the electronics industry which is usually in the position of a frontrunner.

... too little flexibility

On the supply side, European firms encounter comparatively as unfavourable conditions as their most important world market competitors. The financing conditions are worse for the most part, and working hours not flexible enough to permit an optimum utilization of the extremely capital-intensive production facilities. Both are home-made locational disadvantages and cannot be blamed on the Japanese. If work in Japanese firms is longer or more flexible, they cannot be criticized for that. It is our own fault that reductions in working hours are not more closely linked to a greater flexibility in working hours. The Japanese are not to blame for that.

It is a failed wage-scale policy when the same working hours apply for highly-specialized engineers as for unskilled workers. In the end, the success of any society depends on how it uses its most productive workers. In Japan, this is clearly in production. Japan is a producer, not a service or consumer, society. Germany and Japan are similar in this respect, even if great differences exist otherwise. In the US, the service industry attracts the most capable workers. Here is where most money can be earned, and here is where the college graduates who dream of being millionaires at 30 want to work. That perhaps explains why some stress product quality and improvement and others specialize more in service. Europe appears to lie somewhere in the middle, but nowhere does it enjoy a prominent position, neither in hardware nor in software.

... too little market potential

There are large differences in company structures between Japan and the US on the one hand and Europe on the other. American and above all Japanese firms are integrated vertically, ie, they form a closed technological loop, from components to equipment to software. This carries considerable strategic advantage: there are no problems with differing standards. The best example is IBM, which for years has been able to establish its standards on the world level because it was the world's leading computer manufacturer. Nowhere are European electronics firms absolute market leaders and they must adapt as a result to the changing market conditions. That is also a result of the lack of a single market.

Moreover, in contrast to machinery, European electronics firms apparently find it more difficult to convert technical know-how quickly into marketable products. Not the least important reason for this is that the contacts between users and producers are not close enough to allow effective interaction in the market. If one knows only generally what the customer wants, one must spend correspondingly more time introducing products to the market or miss the boat entirely. Every innovation ought to begin with a user consultation but in Europe the direction is usually the opposite: first the great technical invention and then the thoughts about whether the customer needs it. The answer is often a disappointing 'No'.

WHY WE NEED A EUROPEAN ELECTRONICS INDUSTRY

Considering the significance of the electronics industry, the crucial industrial–political question poses itself: can the Community afford to attain at most a middle position in these key areas? The radical answer is: if we no longer produce semiconductors in Europe, we will simply buy them from Japan and the US. Has the US not practically abdicated in the area of entertainment electronics and do

Americans not still watch TV? The American film studios are in the hands of Japanese entertainment giants, but it is always the American movie stars who get the most Oscars. Can one quietly sit back and leave everything else to competition? Certainly not, because if one does not want to live on one's capital, the imported TV sets and movie licence fees have to be paid for out of one's own exports. Weaknesses in some areas have to be offset by strengths in others. If electronics as a base technology is really the raw material for growth and productivity, one must not simply let the key fall out of one's hand. The difference between television sets and semiconductors is that we can live quite well without the former, but we can no longer live without the latter.

... to avoid technological dependencies

Whoever has not mastered modern electronics finds himself dependent on others. It is not only a question of supplies, for these dependencies also exist in other branches such as energy or mineral raw materials, and we also manage there. The deciding factor is the dependence on foreign know-how, because the most important factor for economic strength and international competitiveness in the countries lacking raw materials is mastery of the most modern technologies. To increase a country's prosperity, the enterprises must be productive and raise that productivity. How does that happen? Only by constantly improving quality, refining products, finding new manufacturing processes and further developing professional skills. It is not a matter of static efficiency but rather of constant dynamic improvement. Electronics plays a decisive role in this area.

Lacking expertise in key technologies would have negative impact on the total network of economic activity. The loss of know-how on the part of suppliers and lack of chances for user-tailored solutions represent only the tip of the iceberg. Here it is clear that judgements are required in terms of not only sector-specific interests but also total economic necessity. This has been the case in Japan and the US for a long time. Both countries have an active industrial policy for strengthening the technological base, but the emphasis is divided differently between military and civil applications.

The civil initiative has shown itself to be clearly in front. The thesis that military research also has a large civil application and brings the entire country to technological heights is no longer true today. Not only can considerably more money be earned with CD players, video recorders or personal computers than with fighter aircraft or missiles. There are hardly any civil by-products from military research any more, but modern precision weapons are increasingly dependent on microelectronics, which develop much more rapidly under public competition than under military secrecy. Japan's path has proved to be more successful. This is sufficient proof that it is not a question of a simple planning model because planned economies have failed miserably on all fronts.

THE EC MUST REMAIN TECHNOLOGICALLY STRONG

Industrial policy must contribute to improving the competitiveness of the European electronics industry. The question is simply, how? Old mistakes must not be repeated. The raw material idea must not lead to an exaggerated self-sufficiency attitude. The failed EC agricultural policy is certainly no example for electronics. Further, the magic words 'key industry' must not lead automatically to a claim for subsidy. I therefore would consider it dangerous that the Community could, with a qualified majority, make aid decisions for so-called 'strategic' future projects, as some member countries want to write into the new EC treaty. The industrial policy of the past does not help us with electronics. The new concept must consist of replacing independence by interdependence. Europe can not and must not produce everything, but Europe must at least be a technologically equal partner. The single market is not intended to replace the world market, but it can help to better prepare the European companies for it.

... BUT DO NOT CROWN ANY 'EUROCHAMPIONS'

The Japanese successes must not lead to the false conclusion that Europe, too, desperately needs a MITI. The challenge of Japanese firms does not call for the EC Commission to act as a 'company forge'. The idea of entering the technological competition with a single 'Eurochampion' has, in my opinion, little chance for success. Without competition in one's own market, the only result is a technological giant which will never stand on its own but rather remain on public intravenous feeding. Industrial policy cannot be conducted using the motto, 'If a blind man carries a cripple, neither falters'. European firms must not be forced into merger just to enable larger returns to scale. Each must seek the partner which suits it best. National pride would be totally out of place here.

Industrial policy cannot relieve enterprises of their responsibility, but rather can play a subsidiary and complementary role. The development of competitiveness in electronics enterprises remains primarily the task of the enterprises themselves. This is especially true in the light of the new opportunities which the single market offers. What is needed is long-term thinking, an increase in productivity, customer contact, an ability to adapt quickly and an intensified willingness to cooperate internationally. Especially in the electronics area, the ability to convert technology into new products has paramount importance. Industrial policy however cannot carry the enterprises to market – they must get there on their own.

This market-directed concept of industrial policy is in no way uncontroversial in the Community. Some want considerably more. Assistance for concrete projects is demanded so that electronics can play to the end its role as a key, future-oriented industry. The point is made, not entirely unjustifiably, that our trading partners define the electronics industry as 'strategic' and conduct literal market conquest campaigns, sometimes under government control. The conclusion is: block off the outside and actively support Community industries. That sounds logical but it does not help us get any further.

EUROPEAN CONTENDERS MUST COOPERATE MORE STRONGLY

There is no shortage of instructive examples of where establishing industrial wildlife preserves can lead. But should not the EC Commission at least take an active role in merging European enterprises? This demand seems at first glance to bear something for the electronics sector. Primarily in the information technology field, European enterprises are, measured on a world scale, rather small and maybe too small. IBM is larger than all other European competitors combined. In semiconductors the outlook is similar. Here, the European manufacturers would have to double their turnover in order to be at least half the size of the market leader. Europe's semiconductor manufacture might lie below the critical level for economical production. The call for mergers at the European level suggests itself. Although experience shows that mere size is not a guarantee for success, it can be seen that, especially in semiconductors, capital requirements are extremely high. A certain company size can be indispensable for success in the world market.

But what is the conclusion? Certainly not that the European firms must on all accounts merge into conglomerates in order to fight

Japanese and American superiority. A merger is not necessarily the complete answer. The merged entities must also fit together and complement one another in meaningful ways. That was seen clearly in the Siemens-Nixdorf merger case. This merger must first be 'digested' from an entrepreneurial aspect before the anticipated synergy effects can occur. The enterprises must therefore assume the initiative and the risk. They are in the best position to determine possible advantages from a merger or a cooperation. Political stirrups are not needed in this case.

But that does not mean that industrial policy should not facilitate cooperation among the firms. In mergers and cooperative agreements, one must consider that the global market for electronics has only a few large participants, whose number probably will continue to shrink in the future. The world market is becoming more and more the relevant market. European cooperation is no value in and of itself, but rather it must stand the test of the market. Cooperative agreements must be oriented toward the needs of the companies and not toward political wish lists. Multiple forms of cooperation and internetting, which could all be useful in the end are conceivable. Thus, the common European research in the framework of the 'JESSI' programme does not prevent Siemens, as one of the JESSI participants, from at the same time engaging with IBM in research for the 64-megabit chip. Furthermore, both partners want to manufacture 16-megabit DRAMs in France. Even if everything does not operate under a purely European flag, it serves to keep advanced know-how in Europe for Europe. This example should set a precedent.

STRATEGIC ALLIANCES STRENGTHEN MARKET ACCESS

Even today, complete autonomy in every area of electronics is no longer possible. Properly selected partners, however, can complement each other meaningfully. In particular, the area of entertainment electronics shows that such global strategic alliances are often unavoidable. In this case, it was not necessarily the better technology that won out but rather the stronger alliance with the better software potential. This was clearly seen in the fate of VD2000 and Betamax with respect to VHS. Even the largest can no longer have their own way in everything. That was true for the music cassette and the CD, and it also holds true for the digital compact cassette (DCC), the mini CD, as well as the interactive CD (CDA). Moreover, new recording media require new recording techniques, so that it is not enough simply to offer outstanding playback equipment. On the other hand, the best technology is useless if no software is available for it.

World-encircling alliances can form a decisive competitive advantage in introducing technical innovations on the market. In order to prevail in the world market, market introduction must be massive, rapid and accompanied by a large advertising campaign. Here, the window of opportunity must not be missed: in rapid technological development, an advantage can often be utilized on a large scale only for a brief time. The example of the digital audio cassette shows the consequences of what holding back modern technology can have on market chances.

An indispensable factor for the success of international cooperation is the equality of the partners. A cooperation with one-sided technological dependence leads in the short or long term to economic dependence and is thereby often the prelude to a 'soft' takeover. What may be acceptable for individual enterprises would be fatal for the total European electronics industry. International cooperation with European partners must not only pave the way into the single market. The call for 'market access in exchange for new technology' may suit the developing countries, which need foreign help to establish their own industries, but it does not apply to 'mature' economies, which are represented in world competition by more and more specialized and advanced industries.

HORIZONTAL INITIATIVE IN THE ELECTRONICS INDUSTRY TOO

European industrial policy must help to strengthen the technological base in the Community in order to ensure cooperation on an equal-to-equal basis. The horizontal initiative with the objective of creating the best possible conditions for investment and production in Europe is therefore the correct one for electronics. On the demand side it is primarily a question of developing a European infrastructure for electronic services, while on the supply side the creation of a solid technological foundation, the development of European standards and the improvement of training and continuing education are most important. The creation of a trans-European net for the communications area is part of a proposal of the Commission for a European infrastructure. The single market cannot function correctly without such a net. An automated telecommunications internetting of the administrative centres of the individual member countries is needed. We do not want to establish new centralistic administrative structures in the single market. But the elimination of border controls requires a closer cooperation of the national authorities.

... through internetting of European authorities

Everything which is examined and stamped at border checkpoints must be accomplished by other means after 1992. That affects not only police and customs but also veterinary inspections and tax authorities. The national administrative centres must therefore be more closely internetted, so that the single market leaves behind no security loopholes or opens up chances for fraud. This can only be the first step. In a follow-on step, other institutions such as health authorities, transportation firms and research institutes must also be interconnected. The single market will generate new information requirements and cooperation needs. The communications nets required for this have been largely non-existent up to this point. Capacity is neither sufficient, nor are the nets compatible with each other. This must change in the single market. New impulses can be anticipated from stronger integration of electronics in the structural policy of the Community. Specific Community initiatives such as STRIDE, START, TELEMATIQUE, and PRISMA, are to create a favourable framework for development and distribution of new technologies, particularly in the small- and middle-class enterprises as well as in the structurally weak areas of the Community.

... through more market-sensitive research and development

A second task of industrial policy consists of retaining and strengthening a solid technological foundation that is essential, especially for the electronics industry. The Community programmes ESPRIT and JESSI serve that purpose. These projects must be continued and expanded. Overall, the technology support of the Community should concentrate on a few areas of activity with broad impact. Even in the research stage, work must be more user-oriented. Working together with users must be intensified. Research aid in the electronics area cannot be limited to the pre-competition phase. A certain market sensitivity is simply required in order to be the first on the market with a technological innovation. That is true for consumer goods as well as for fundamental technologies and the newest superchip. Electronics is short-lived, and whoever is not the first in the market must live with lower prices or even ruinous competition.

In electronics therefore, the strict distinction between foundation research and applications research can no longer be made. As soon as a theoretical problem has been solved, competition for production capacity begins. A focal point for semiconductor research lies justifiably in processor technology. The 'factory of the future' is certainly worthy of support. The only problem is what pot it should come out of. Funds would be available in the framework of regional assistance, and the assistance rates are quite attractive. The question is simply whether the electronics companies are ready to locate primary technologies, which have not been tested anywhere, in structurally weak areas.

... through transfer of technological know-how

The electronics industry is dependent on highly-qualified researchers, engineers and workers, and these are not available everywhere. Under sonorous names, the Commission has for years offered special programmes and initiatives for training and continuing education in the area of 'new technologies' (for example, DELTA, COMETT, FORCE and EUROFORM). It has also presented objective-oriented recommendations for steps to improve vocational training. A further industrial policy concept is measures for supporting the mobility of researchers as well as a better internetting of universities and industry. This should promote not only the bringing together of a critical mass of know-how but also a better utilization of valuable research resources. There is, therefore, activity in the research area, but this is not yet true on the same scale for the users. Here, good user electronics training would be extremely important.

It is not only a question of enabling users to employ products of the electronics industry. Rather, they must have the ability to discover new application areas and combinations. Only in this way can they contribute to further technological development. It is also true in this case, that the interplay between offerors and users occur early, intensively and intelligently. Application intelligence and production intelligence must be in a dynamic equilibrium. Training and continuing education must also not stop at the higher management levels; otherwise, advanced information and telecommunications technology will find little application in new management and production systems.

... through opening of the markets

Liberalizing the telecommunications services in the EC will strongly accelerate the development and growth of this sector and in turn the equipment industry. With the opening of the procurement markets of the telecommunications sector, which have up till now been closed, the Community has finally introduced international competition in this important electronics area. This must not lead, however, to structural competitive disadvantages with respect to Japanese and American companies, which can bid on public procurements without EC firms being permitted the same competitive conditions in their domestic markets. It is not enough to point out that network operators in the US and Japan are private companies and as such are not subject to the same regulations as the government-owned companies in Europe. To the extent that American and Japanese telecommunications companies possess exclusive rights, which exclude others from operating their own networks, similar rules must apply to them as to government-owned companies in the EC. Much would be accomplished if the American and Japanese monopolies would at least use international standards, so that the procurement cartels between parents and subsidiaries would at last be broken up. This is an important topic for bilateral discussions between the EC, Japan and the US.

... through protection of intellectual property

European industrial policy also consists of representing the interests of European electronics firms in important foreign markets. The classical instruments of subsidies, protective tariffs or self-limitation agreements lose more and more significance in the light of the increasing interdependence in electronics. On the other hand, the protection of intellectual property, for example, is becoming increasingly more important, even if it is not directly in the spotlight. Thus, the enormous investments in semiconductor technology require sufficient protection of the chip's inner workings, ie, the semiconductor architecture. The Community was the first of the large manufacturing blocs to create this protection, and it can be expected that the EC laws will assume an important vanguard role in this difficult legal area.

The affected industry was relatively late to recognize the great industrial-political significance of computer software, but then it did so emphatically. Hardly any other EC law was subjected to such heavy wrangling over each individual formulation. What initially appears as a technical explanation quickly reveals itself on closer examination as a basic direction-setting of industrial policy. The deciding question is no less than to what extent experience should be protected in order not to break the will to innovate. If intellectual property is protected too strongly, economic dynamism is hindered because imitators are forced to enter too late. On the other hand, too little protection means that one is no longer ready to invest in expensive computer software. How much is the competition permitted to peer into a program's internals so that open systems are possible but a competitor does not obtain any undeserved advantages? Discussion of such questions is not just for lawyers because that is primarily industrial policy.

HIGH-DEFINITION TELEVISION AS A NEW TECHNOLOGY OF THE FUTURE?

Much money is also at stake with high-definition television (HDTV). The fact that Europe today has a competitive television industry is attributable not least to the fact that high-quality picture standards were available for the leap into the colour television age with PAL and SECAM. In order to remain competitive for the next television generation, HDTV, the Community is pursuing a multi-level strategy: in the 'EUREKA 95' programme, the EC has given a decided push to the technological development. Europe has shown here that it is very much in a position to make up for being in technological arrears to Japan, and this in an astoundingly short period of time. The next step is the definition of the transmission standard, which will legally pave the way to flicker-free pictures.

CONFLICTING OBJECTIVES BETWEEN CONSUMER AND PRODUCER INTERESTS

In this respect, European industrial policy finds itself in a predicament. If the new transmission standard is to be implemented quickly, this is possible only through direct manipulation, for example by requiring that the receivers contain an appropriate tuner or that new programme broadcasters be forced from the very beginning to transmit using only the new standard, although there may be no programmes for it. A chaotic confusion of the systems would be just as expensive for the television viewer and would moreover delay, if not fully impede, the implementation of a European standard. If the EC delays a decision much longer, it is possible that the currently-favoured analogue system will be obsolete before it is even introduced, since work is being undertaken in the US and in Europe on standards for digital HDTV transmission. At the present time, no one can say whether the delay of this decision represents a true competitive disadvantage or whether it may even pave the way for a truly future-oriented technology. Whatever the political decision may be, it must be guaranteed at any rate that the manufacturers can supply sufficient hardware and the stations have sufficient air time.

The last problem concerns the programming which must be HDTV-compatible. It will be interesting to see when the initial programmes in HDTV quality are transmitted in Europe and who supplies the receivers for this new television generation. But even after that, much remains to be done. The optimum utilization of the medium HDTV will quickly encounter the limits of present television receiver technology. The advantages of high resolution are heavily dependent on screen size. Since giant-screen sets may fit through the main entrance to the White House but rarely through the front door of the average apartment, the future lies in the flat screen. That is a sort of picture-on-the-wall that can be used not only in private homes but also in physicians' waiting rooms or adult education classes. In developing such screens, which also have applications in many areas other than television (for example, computers), Europe is still somewhat behind.

HDTV IS ONLY THE BEGINNING

Technology is dynamic and must also be considered dynamic by the public. Even with an advanced technology such as analogue HDTV, one must look further into the future. This means the need for the parallel development of a fully-digital HDTV system, as is underway in Project EUREKA 256 for defining a standard for digital HDTV transmission and in the framework of the RACE programme for signal compression. In the light of the considerable research efforts undertaken in the triad countries, the key to success lies in global alliances and in the development of digital world standards. Today, a successful strategy must stand on many legs. In the case of HDTV, it is a question not only of which pictures will appear in the future on screens, but also who manufactures the recording and receiving equipment. That would be reason enough to exert oneself, since there is a mega market waiting for HDTV manufacturers. Experts estimate the market volume for the necessary conversion alone at over DM 15 billion. But that is not everything. Almost more important is the fact that HDTV is a new key technology with a far-reaching significance for many important areas such as medicine, education, graphics and printing.

HDTV is an outstanding example of the numerous interdependencies which industrial policy has to deal with. Naturally, one can simply lay one's hands in one's lap and trust that the market will regulate things. The market however is dependent on political signals to make correct decisions. Certainly, standards are developed in competition; but television transmission depends on a certain political stimulus. Each country can afford its own plug, but a television is considerably more complicated than an electric razor. With the introduction of colour television, Germany decided on PAL, France on SECAM. This market splintering brought neither much advantage because Japanese manufacturers for a long time have produced sets for both systems. For the television of the future, the opportunity exists for border-free European television, but that requires a dependable framework. Each investment in a particular television standard costs the economy billions – billions which are lost if governments decide otherwise or other standards prevail on the market. Whoever has the standards also has the market. For electronics in particular, industrial policy cannot simply avoid this already-mentioned standards maxim. That would be too easy.

10

Creating a Consensus: The Biotechnology and Pharmaceutical Industry

The pharmaceutical industry is among those which suffer the most under the present splintering of the European market. This may seem bewildering at first, since this branch is one of the most internationally competitive and sales-intensive in the EC. The European pharmaceutical industry is the world's largest drug manufacturer with 60 per cent of worldwide exports and 40 per cent of all new preparations. At the same time, the branch is one of the most research-intensive, where 90 per cent of the research expenditures are financed privately. The pharmaceutical industry does not ask for subsidies or protection from outside. From an industrial policy perspective, this branch is clearly a model child: strong in sales, research-intensive and competitive. Yet, all is not right in the world.

For one thing, acceptance problems trouble the pharmaceutical industry. The problems are especially onerous in biotechnology, but the public also reacts with extreme sensitivity even to common preparations. This is entirely understandable since pharmaceuticals affect people directly, whether it is the expected healing power or the feared side effects. There are usually emotions at play in any discussion of pharmaceuticals, and not infrequently a genuine reluctance to invest arises, which leads to relocation to foreign countries. Secondly, re-structuring is forced by the higher competitive intensity caused by increasing expenditures for research and development, rising marketing costs, worldwide cost-saving measures and, not least, the realization of the single market. For both reasons, the pharmaceutical industry is knocking on the door in Brussels asking for industrial-political assistance.

NATIONAL BORDERS ARE A HINDRANCE

The pharmaceutical market today is a global market. New products are essential for market success. Constantly rising research and development expenditures for developing new active ingredients pay off only if the market is widespread. As soon as a product is ready for the market, approval in the most important markets of the triad must be obtained as quickly as possible. The inefficient and time-consuming approval procedures in the individual member countries are a serious problem for the pharmaceutical industry in the EC. Before a new medication can be introduced in the market, companies must wait on average four to five years for its approval. This is in addition to the eight to ten years required for laboratory tests and trials after the patent application is filed. The effective patent protection for drugs boils down to only a few years. The customary term of 20 years begins with the patent application, but the product finds economic utility only after market approval. A supplementary protection certificate which will guarantee drugs the usual patent protection by discounting the time spent waiting for the approval is therefore planned. The shorter this amortization period, the lower the willingness to innovate. Patent protection therefore has a strong industrial-political significance, which has at times been underestimated.

The European pharmaceutical industry is one of the most heavily regulated branches in the Community. From approval to marketing to price setting, practically everything related to drugs is prescribed in the smallest detail and subjected to national supervision. The only problem is that each member country has its own regulations, and for this reason there is little international pharmaceutical trade. The regional markets are dominated largely by the local-national pharmaceutical companies, and market access for foreign manufacturers succeeds best by taking over a local producer. This is the principal reason for the take-over fever presently raging in the pharmaceutical industry.

As long as the pharmaceutical industry was still making good profits, there was no special interest in the single market. Attention was directed entirely on the national health authorities, on which one is dependent in many ways, whether for market approval for new medications or for administrative price fixing in the framework of national reimbursement systems. But this narrow alliance between drug manufacturers and the national health system is gradually becoming more brittle. Not only is the pharmaceutical industry coming under increasing political pressure almost all over the world to cut costs in healthcare, but the realization of the single market also changes the strategic starting position. The branch cannot expect drug prices to increase very much in the future. The pharmaceutical manufacturers too will soon be forced into direct competition with each other. Out of 12 regional sub-markets, a homogeneous European pharmaceutical market will arise, which, although it improves the starting position for worldwide operation, will permit new competitors to enter the well-established regional markets.

THE SINGLE MARKET IS CHANGING THE COMPETITIVE SITUATION

According to professional estimates (Cecchini report), the cost-cutting potential based on the single market lies between 0.5 and 1.6 per cent. This estimate might be on the low side. Overcapacity in production for the pharmaceutical industry is about 60 per cent. Considerable pressure for rationalization will be triggered not only by continuing cost-cutting pressure but also by Community-wide approval for medications. National borders will no longer protect the pharmaceutical industry but rather give the drug manufacturers a false sense of security. The large differences in drug prices can hardly remain in the single market. Either manufacturers will set new prices, or drug distributors will take advantage of the price differences. Such parallel imports however are not the result of the single market but of peculiarities in drug price setting, which is based on peculiarities of the national reimbursement systems and not on economic considerations.

The first building blocks for a uniform single market for medications have already been laid. The criteria and approval procedures for introducing drugs to the market have been gradually harmonized within the Community. From 1992 onwards, there will be a uniform market for all industrially manufactured drugs. Here, a clear distinction between non-prescription and prescription drugs is important. Risks of various types require different treatment, for example in advertising. Public advertising should be permitted for non-prescription remedies but not for prescription medications. Advertising is one of the most sensitive topics in the single market. On the one hand, different advertising guidelines in various countries often have a trade-hindering effect. If advertising is not permitted for a product, it will have difficulty finding its way to consumers, and that is true especially for the single market where attachment to generally known brand names is not yet possible. On the other hand, the danger in harmonizing advertising guidelines is agreeing on the lowest common denominator, and that can mean national advertising bans are extended to the entire Community. The single market will then serve only as a vehicle for pushing through other, often arbitrary, objectives.

DIFFERING CONTROLS FOR DRUG ADVERTISING

For freely-marketable products, advertising must be permitted on general principle. We have adhered to this principle, at least for drugs. The only prohibited public advertising is that for prescription drugs, as is true today in all member countries. That is also completely correct, since in this case the physician and not the patient decides whether and which medications should be taken. For the non-prescription remedies, which make up about a fifth of all medications on the market, the patient makes the decision. Due to the small dosage for these remedies, there is no prescription requirement. Here too, advertising contributes to consumer education because making a decision requires that one knows which natural preparations and other remedies exist on the market and what purpose they serve. Health risks must not be down-played in permitted drug advertising. Advertising and packaging do not need to contain every warning notice. The internal directions-for-use sheet is in many instances a better means of warning against side effects or abuse. For this reason, an obligatory directions sheet for all medications is to be introduced in the Community. This is reasonable in my opinion, even if it generates additional costs. Otherwise, confidence in the single market cannot be established.

Critics see in advertising an attack on the sovereignty of the individual because it allegedly seduces the purchaser to buy a product. A basic criticism of a market economy reveals itself herein: the consumer is seen as a victim of the market process, not as a control element. But quality does not prevail on its own. Of course, the purpose of advertising is not simply education; advertising intends to seduce. But that is no reason for a total advertising ban. Even for remedies, new high-quality preparations with fewer side effects and better tolerance – for people with allergies, for example – still appear in the market. Advertising for these products must be permitted. How else are they to be noticed on fully-stocked shelves?

PERPETUAL SEARCH FOR BETTER SOLUTIONS

Even if one is of the opinion that there are already enough pain and sedative medications and tablets for motion sickness and stomach or intestinal ailments, research and development on new preparations cannot be impeded. A determination of need for new medications should not be required because that would inhibit the search for better solutions. We must never give up this search. Everything can be refined or improved. If society stops looking for new, improved methods, even if only to better fight certain headaches, it will lose its economic dynamism and, worse still, become inhumanely paralysed. Freezing of the *status quo* in reality means that some presume to dominate others by prescribing what is good and what is bad, what is defective and what is superfluous. To this extent, our attitude towards advertising allows deep insights into our own view of man, which serves as a model.

Despite uniform advertising and packaging regulations, it will still not be possible in the future to offer the identical-format drug within the entire Community. This failure is due to the fact that warning notices must be written in the local language. Medications must therefore be re-packaged as necessary. But there is no way around that. If warnings are not to fail to serve their purpose they must be understandable for the consumer. There are language limitations to uniformity in the Community, and these must not be violated. Invariably industry does not correctly understand this. It is often overlooked that the single market only opens the legal gates for the free, unencumbered trade of goods, but does not establish complete unity. Cultural distinctions in the individual member countries must continue to be respected in the future. Each EC citizen has the right to be addressed in his own language when it concerns his health or safety.

AN EMPHASIS ON SELF-MEDICATION

The basic premise for self-medication will be further supported by the single market. For the first time, non-prescription drugs will be defined as an independent category with special regulations.

Furthermore, advertising will play a role in bringing self-medication closer to the consumers, who until now have remained largely under the oversight of the public health authorities. The governmental share of total drug expenditures is between 61 per cent in Denmark and 78 per cent in Great Britain. The deductible plays only a minor role everywhere, in contrast to Switzerland for example, where only half of drug costs are reimbursed. Even in the Community, the deductible must take on more importance in order to limit the increasing drug expenditures, which already make up between 0.67 per cent and 1.9 per cent of the gross national product. In this respect, self-medication drugs can perform important pace-setting functions because they promote health as well as reduce costs.

AN EC SYSTEM FOR DRUG APPROVAL

To support trust in the single market, it is important that all approved pharmaceutical products be tested according to the same rules. The single market cannot exist without its own administrative structures. However, bureaucratic centralism cannot be permitted to arise therefrom. For many today, Brussels represents an over-zealous super-bureaucracy that intends to regulate and inspect everything, but this really is not true at all. What many do not know is that the EC has no administrative substructure of its own, something which in many cases considerably hampers the application of Community law. Criticism of the EC proceeds in two different directions. While some complain about the existing control and inspection gaps and demand more stringent Community controls on food, waste or chemicals for example, others place more trust in a national stamp. This lack of trust also shows the lack of transparency of legislation in the Community: the Commission proposes but the Council decides. The execution of Council resolutions is primarily the responsibility of the member countries but the Commission is responsible in public for misuse and dissatisfaction. The EC must live with the image that more is demanded of it than can be expected. This confidence gap desperately needs to be closed, so that the single market also has citizen acceptance.

... EQUAL RULES FOR EQUAL RISKS

For the approval of new drugs, dependability and confidence must be coupled with economic efficiency. Research and development for a new preparation today costs on average DM 400 million. A company therefore has already spent this much on basic research and testing when it applies for approval. Every year, 60 new decision-requiring substances press themselves onto the pharmaceutical market. Until now, this happens in the Community chiefly in the framework of a consultation procedure. Applications filed in the individual member countries are forwarded concurrently to the Community health authorities, so that a mutual recognition of market approval can occur without long delays. This country-level testing procedure costs the member countries a total of about DM 400 million a year; coordination costs at the Community level amount to only one hundredth of this sum. At least the efficiency aspect seems satisfied. Unfortunately, however, this consultation procedure between the national governments has decided weaknesses, which make it advisable to look for better solutions.

Until now, no Community-wide approval has been achieved within the framework of the consultation procedure. The principle of mutual recognition fails regularly due to the ambition of the national approving authorities to review application papers once again in detail. The readiness to accept the judgement of other authorities is in this case very low. In the future as well, decisions on simple medications are to be made on the national level, but the consultation procedure employed up till now is to be replaced by a Community 'clearing', so that in cases of doubt a majority can decide on the Community-wide approval of a given medication.

Applications for approval of new active ingredients are concentrated within a few countries. While in these cases the approval process is lengthy, in other countries the administrative structures and scientific competence for smoothly guaranteeing mutual recognition are non-existent. In practically no case are the prescribed approval periods adhered to. A first alternative would be the establishment of an American-style 'European Food and Drug Agency', which would decide on the legal requirements for new medications as well as on their approval. The US authority (FDA) enjoys an outstanding international reputation. Preparations tested and approved by the FDA have outstanding marketing opportunities worldwide, since an approval for the American market also opens doors to other markets. This is also true because government inspectors follow the entire development process of a new ingredient practically from the beginning, so that in each phase close contact exists with the approving authorities. Costly investment errors are thereby largely avoided because judgement criteria are known and can be taken into account by industry from the start.

Nevertheless, the US model is suitable only in a limited sense for an EC approval procedure.

... BUT DO NOT CREATE A EUROPEAN SUPER AUTHORITY

The American FDA has a personnel strength of about 3,000 specialized employees. The same number of experts is also available in the member countries in the Community but they are not as well utilized, since the same approval application has to undergo multiple examinations. This is really a waste of resources. A central EC health authority, however, would not be a reasonable solution since its establishment would require too much time and the necessary professional expertise is not present at the Community level. The example of the controversy over the location of the German capital shows how difficult it is to move civil servants. This would be even more difficult to accomplish in Europe. Instead of a new super authority, the EC is proposing a relatively small European agency with only 100 permanent employees, which would, in close cooperation with the national health authorities, examine new medicines according to the three scientific criteria of safety, quality and efficiency. The processing time for applications would thereby be reduced from the present four to five years to 300 days. This would be a huge advance, with considerable industrial-political weight, since it is well known that time is money.

The planned medicine agency is primarily a scientific organization. In contrast to the American FDA, it would have no decision making authority of its own. The member countries still have the last word on Community approval for pharmaceutical products. In the case of common medications, they will continue to decide directly in the future, but in close cooperation with the other member countries, so that each new medication can be made available Community-wide from the first day forward. For the few highly-effective substances on the other hand, an EC-wide regulation will be sought. The scientific recommendations of the medicine agency serve thereby as a basis for a decision. As a rule, there should never be a reason to deviate from this in any way. In some cases a political decision may be needed, especially when ethical issues are involved. The industry would of course prefer that decisions would be made only on the basis of the three scientific criteria, but government cannot be satisfied with such a 'notary public' function in which the scientific recommendation simply receives the recognition of the legislative body. This would mean blindly assuming responsibility. That is also not in the economic interest because politically unresolved conflicts can quickly become problems for the industry itself. Biotechnology is a frightening example of that.

BIOTECHNOLOGY IS AN IMPORTANT TECHNOLOGY OF THE FUTURE

'Biotechnology' is neither an independent industry nor a product. Rather, it is a method which will be employed more intensively in the future for development and production of drugs, agricultural products, food products and other goods required on a daily basis, as well as for industrial applications. Biotechnology in no way represents a new method. Even today, numerous products have undergone biotechnical processing or are of biologic origin, without stirring up any problems. The market for biotechnological products in the narrow sense, ie, excluding food and drink produced by fermentation, amounts in the Community to an estimated DM 15 billion. A tripling of this turnover is expected until the year 2000. All of this shows that biotechnology has outstanding prospects for the future, provided that the remaining acceptance problems can be resolved to reasonable satisfaction.

INCREASED EMPHASIS ON THE USEFULNESS OF BIOTECHNOLOGY

The usefulness of biotechnology is undisputed. Products manufactured using biotechnology, such as vaccines, human insulin for treating diabetes and above all cancer treatment medications have already saved many human lives. The newest hope is an AIDS preparation which is derived using biotechnology. Work is also being conducted in the development of drought-resistant plants, as well as plants with higher resistance to insect feeding and viral or fungal infections. The developing countries have particular interest in this area. These countries also have a strong interest in improved methods for animal breeding. The industrial countries can expect considerable advances in environmental issues from biotechnology, for example improved waste water treatment, treatment of hazardous waste or new plastic and packing materials with improved biodegradability. Applications for biotechnology are just as many-sided as they are promising, but in public the possible dangers and ethical conflicts are discussed almost exclusively. Creating hysteria is easy because hardly anyone knows what biotechnology really can do, and most understand it to mean primarily genetic manipulation on humans, ie, creating babies in a test tube. The usefulness is discussed only in professional circles, and that makes it difficult to arrive at a balanced range of opinion.

DO NOT PLAY DOWN RISKS, BUT ALSO DO NOT EXAGGERATE

Industrial policy also has the task of contributing to dealing with technological risks reasonably. Here it is not a question of appeasement or merely obtaining authentication papers. Industry does not take enough trouble when it attempts to force government into such a role. Politics must solve conflicts and balance interests, not simply cover them over with words. Prejudice must also be taken seriously. In biotechnology, the concern for genetic manipulation as well as for safety precautions in the production area is especially important. Acceptable answers are needed in both areas in order to make biotechnology acceptable to the public. The discussion on critical aspects of biotechnology must be carried out seriously and should in no case be considered only as a means to an end. The credibility test rests in public participation in legislation and later in approval procedures for research and production facilities. In both cases, transparency must be established so that biotechnology is placed on a solid acceptance base.

The security aspects of biotechnology have to a large extent been resolved with satisfaction in the Community. That is also recognized by environmental protectionists. The guidelines passed with respect to labour and environmental protection ensure that there is no danger from biological work materials and the release of genetically modified organisms into the environment. Strict safety precautions have been prescribed for both areas, and these have served to strengthen confidence in biotechnology. Thus, before release for research and development purposes, an environmental impact test must be conducted. This must also be adhered to when sector-specific guidelines are issued for individual biotechnological products. But such a special market approval is not required for every biotechnological product. For biotechnologically produced 'novel food', an approval requirement exists only if it contains new chemical substances or genetic modifications, or if the new food substance is particularly problematic with respect to toxicity, tolerance or nutrition. Biotechnology is not dangerous in itself: it always depends on the special risk.

If a special approval for biotechnological products cannot for risk reasons be dispensed with, all safety and environmental aspects must be examined, by the responsible approving authority if possible. Costly and time-consuming double examinations by various authorities should be avoided as much as possible. There must be no wrestling for authority at the expense of the applicant. That is what is meant by the concept 'one door, one key': one application, one permanent approving authority and one approval for the entire Community. That would be the ideal to strive for from an industrial policy standpoint. This basic principle is already planned for application to biotechnologically produced insecticides, and the Commission is striving toward approval of new medications which have been manufactured on a biotechnological basis.

THE ETHICAL DIMENSION MUST BE CONSIDERED

The evaluation of the ethical dimension of biotechnology suffers strongly from inexact language. Almost everything which is in any way politically controversial is considered to be an 'ethical' issue. To a certain extent, ethics form the moral background for political decisions. Ethical issues arise especially where human identity and future are concerned. Depending on the point of view, this can cover the entire spectrum of the relationship of man to nature. In the present case, such basic ethical issues concern primarily intervention into human reproduction, but the question of whether humans should render plants pest-resistant by implanting them with insect repellent can also be argued on ethical grounds.

There are not always binding answers even for legitimate ethical issues. An 'ethics law', which defines exactly what is ethically permitted or prohibited, would be a contradiction in terms. The openness of society to new questions must be preserved in any case. Whatever is decided today can be changed again tomorrow. Even social values change over time. There are no definitive answers to all ethical issues. The primary question related to biotechnology in ethical affairs is the right to a hearing which is anchored in the law. The Commission intends to establish an advisory body of high-ranking and recognized personalities who will, using the criterion of ethical unobjectionability, examine and vote on all legislative measures passed at the Community level for the biotechnology area. This appears to me to be a sensible step toward making the ethical debate over biotechnology more objective.

NO NEED TEST FOR BIOTECHNOLOGICAL PRODUCTS

Ethical questions must always be considered in biotechnology, not only as an alibi but also as a genuine decision. This particularly affects the research with which the secret of human genes is decoded and possibly manipulated. Humans should not be fashioned from a test tube. On the other hand, ethics play a less important role for most practical biotechnology applications. Health, safety and environmental protection must be guaranteed in every case. This has already been considered in the three classical approval criteria of quality, safety and efficiency. Transparency in purchase decisions must also be guaranteed. The customer must know how the cheese he bought was processed, even if this simply verifies that his personal preferences have been satisfied. No biotechnological product should be banned from the market simply on the basis of its potential economic significance.

This very point is often hidden behind the demand for increased consideration of socio-economic aspects. Such a 'fourth hurdle', which in addition to the aforementioned three traditional approval criteria involves the socio-economic implications of biotechnology in testing, conceals the great danger of a need test: we produce only what we need and what we need, the product manufacturers say, is whatever is currently on the market. Such a *status quo* mentality is poorly compatible with the basic principles of a market economy, in which consumers should decide which products are produced.

Nevertheless, exceptions can exist even here. For example, a safe and environmentally acceptable biotechnological product can be banned from the market to protect the production structures of small farms or to protect traditional varieties. I will not exclude that *a priori*, but a clear decision must be made on an *ad hoc* basis. A biotechnological product must not be rejected as 'unsafe' or 'insufficiently tested' because it is not wanted for completely different reasons. One should in this case openly stand by the decision to reject, so that the product at least can be marketed where it is perhaps more desperately needed. In any case, trade-policy-based irritation is pre-programmed.

The industry has a right to fair treatment. Whoever wants to forbid something should not hide behind scientific claims for protection. That discredits not only science but also government. Whoever seeks only public applause is better advised not to become a politician. The courage to make an unpopular decision is part of politics and this courage is also demanded particularly in biotechnology. However, here it is not the 'No' which requires the most political courage; it is the conditional 'Yes', because it satisfies no one – neither the critics of biotechnology who frequently do not attempt to justify their objections, nor industry which occasionally gives the impression that ethical issues can be solved with a mere reference to endangering international competitiveness. Both are unsatisfactory and are unacceptable to industrial policy.

Part III

BROADENING THE EUROPEAN DIALOGUE

Industrial policy is often identified with actionism which, depending on the point of view, is either criticized as blind and interventionist or praised as an expression of powerful and responsible politics. But the visible hand of industrial policy describes only one, perhaps the less significant, side of industrial-political activity. The other, less spectacular, side consists of recognizing economic malformations in time and searching together with those affected for reasonable solutions. In daily life, practically no one doubts that it makes sense to talk each other. It is one of the greatest advances in cultural evolution that men have learned to use language to solve their problems. Despite man's turning from the club to conversation, personal dialogue with others in business is considered difficult. At any rate, 'dialogue' is extremely rare in the vocabulary of ardent market analysts, where its use is regarded as a government attempt to create a monopoly or seek global control of the economy through indicative planning. That is regrettable, for in this way an important concept for conflict resolution remains unconsidered. Although the market regulates a lot on its own, it also needs direct contact with one another. The market is by no means the only, nor the most efficient, means for making economic decisions. Even the market can be wrong. Besides, not everything can be expressed in monetary terms. In practical life at any rate, people are not always unreservedly ready to subject themselves to anonymous market forces.

ACCEPTANCE OF COMPETITION MUST BE ESTABLISHED POLITICALLY

The blessings of competition and a market economy can be examined philosophically. For concrete applications it is a little more difficult. Markets demand from all participants the readiness to accept competition and its consequences. European businesses must constantly prove their competitiveness in a rapidly changing environment. Businesses which are no longer profitable, or which manufacture products for which there is no buyer, must close. Workers lose their jobs and must look for new work. This unavoidable pressure for structural adaptation grows with international interpenetration. In such situations, the call is quickly heard for the protective hand of the state. National governments come under internal political pressure to ease competitive pressure through subsidies or import restrictions. This will no longer be easy in the single market, however, for the border-spanning freedom of movement of goods and services requires a strict control of assistance and, due to elimination of the border controls, national import restrictions can in fact no longer be upheld. Without the readiness for a fair balance of interests this could develop quickly into an explosive mixture. Only when the single market is realized next year will structural assistance for the poorer member countries be doubled. The opening of markets for structural adaptation is the historical compromise and, following this example, we will have to make many more compromises if we want to achieve the high objectives of full integration.

THE ABILITY TO COMPROMISE WILL DECIDE EUROPE'S STRENGTH

Many will probably ask themselves what compromise has to do with industrial policy. The future strength of Europe depends quite decidedly on the ability of European-level politics to balance interests. If Europe does not overcome its economic and political splintering, it cannot be an equal partner. As a political decision centre, Brussels is not taken seriously by many. The effect of this does not have to be solely disadvantageous. It is considerably more difficult to push through individual interests at the Community level than at a national level. This is due primarily to the basic freedoms of the market economy which are anchored in the EC treaty; but undoubtedly pressure from the next elections is also missing. The interest groups have not organized themselves accordingly, so they do not exert the same pressure on political decisions as in the member countries. This too makes the political discussion in Europe easier.

In Brussels, therefore, it is less difficult to make reasonable decisions, not least because European policy in the capital cities does not enjoy the same rank as the national policies. The astonishment, and sometimes too the rude awakening, is often greater when Brussels once again eliminates privileges, cuts subsidies or strengthens competition. But this description of the advantages of the opaque EC process of developing objectives must on no account be understood as a plea for isolated decisions not arrived at democratically. In Europe as well, decisions about politics must be made in direct contact with those affected.

LOBBYING IS LEGITIMATE AND USEFUL

Competition accelerates not only structural change but it also leads in the single market to structural breaks which are occasionally serious. The opening of markets and competition therefore needs a broad consensus from society. Otherwise, a relapse into old, nationalistic protectionism threatens. It is not enough for a few to support the concept of the single market, that as broad a path as possible must be found through an overlapping dialogue. Whoever poses this argument must occasionally stand ready to be accused of mumbling. But significantly worse than common discussion is simply ignoring the legitimate interests of individual groups. Representing one's own interests is completely legitimate, especially in a market economy. But on the other hand, the government must be clear on the effect its decisions have in daily life. One learns this best through close contact with reality.

In a free society, enterprises and associations must be able to make their problems known so that correct measures can be taken for improving the economic environment. Contact with those affected also serves to avoid, to the greatest extent possible, friction and efficiency-dampening conflicts between governments, businesses, consumer organizations and unions. Cooperation is therefore a contribution to a more efficient political process. I, not least as commissioner for single market affairs, trade and industry, want the enterprises and associations to come to us in a timely way, so that as much expertise as possible, but also as much sensitivity for the respective interests as is necessary, can be introduced into the policy of the Community. This certainly includes a correct, responsible understanding of lobbying. It does not pay to jump on the barricades for every wish of the enterprises or associations. Even the economy must accept that.

NATIONAL EGOISM CAN ONLY HURT

Blind national egoism no longer has any chance of success in the Community, not to mention the Commission. One does not need to step forward in Brussels to represent special interests which are difficult to understand. I can only advise the associations not to use their elbows for every concern, because that in the end does not help anyone and only damages one's own credibility. Constructive dialogue also means assuming responsibility for the whole. For enterprise associations this means that they must help to develop viable alternatives and not merely attempt to force their solution through with a whip. Above all, false illusions must not be nurtured. Nothing damages Europe more than the belief that everything could stay as it is. Not every favourite section of the law deserves to be defended to the end, because even national legal systems are not perfect, even if one has become accustomed to them. The same acclimatization effect will occur in European law too one day. The single market breaks with many old habits, and that is often not so bad.

... BUT AGAINST EUROPEAN CENTRALISM

To the same degree that the single market leads to the opening up of markets and to increased competition, the member countries understandably are worried about the competitiveness of their own industries. Associated with that is the desire to make one's own location more attractive. That is not only understandable but also completely correct. It would be a great mistake to want to form the entire industrial policy of the EC from one casting in Brussels. European competitiveness develops primarily from the different national strengths. We do not need, therefore, industrial-political centralism which flattens all national differences and thereby creates a single European menu. A Europe *à la carte* must continue to be possible from an industrial policy perspective. That guarantees that one's own mistakes can be corrected as rapidly as possible. The success of one is the best stimulus for the others. Coherence in industrial policy does not mean that all member countries must do absolutely the same thing. Even in the future it must be possible to be better than one's partner. But we have to make sure that this 'competition between the systems' takes place in a fair framework.

THE STRENGTH OF LAW, NOT THE LAW OF STRENGTH

Respect for Community law has decisive importance for a peaceful balancing of national interests and assures the independence predominantly of the smaller member countries of the EC, which can more easily defend themselves against protectionist measures before the European Court than in a bilateral contact. The size of a country plays no role in compliance with EC law. But not everything can be accomplished with the sword of the law. Prevention and close cooperation between the member countries and the Commission are just as important, so that, if possible, conflicts do not even arise. Instead of a formal breach-of-contract procedure, an intensive discussion is sufficient in most cases to eliminate the reason for the complaint. Once caught, most member countries are willing to stop discriminatory practices and open their markets. Contract-breaching and assistance-controlling procedures must remain the *ultimo ratio*, just as complaints before the Court are the sensational exception. Court judgements which cannot be enforced by coercive means depend decidedly on their moral authority. It is therefore important to create a climate of mutual trust, so that those who agree to a market opening are the ones who fear loss through stiffer competition or who trust only the stamp of their own inspectors. We must find the suitable forms and institutions for such trust-building dialogue.

A good example for the institutionalized exchange of opinion in the Community is the notification requirements of the member countries for newly-promulgated technical regulations. In this way, the other member countries learn which regulations are planned for introduction. That starts a mutual exchange of information. On the one hand, the notifying country is told even before the regulations become effective whether they are in harmony with Community law or represent a trade hindrance. That avoids irritation later. Aside from that, surprising technical solutions in practical use in other member countries often come to light in this manner. In this way, each learns more about the other and can learn accordingly from experience.

THE EC MUST REMAIN OPEN TO NEW MEMBERS

The EC is not a private club but rather must strive for good neighbourly relations. Each European democracy can in principle become a member of the European Community. Prior to 1993, however, there will be no negotiations concerning an expansion of the EC. New members can be expected in 1995/1996 at the earliest. In the interim, the member candidates must be offered conditions which permit immediate participation in the single market. But even those countries which do not, or do not yet, wish to become a member of the Community must not be disadvantaged by the single market. The EC therefore has offered the EFTA countries an agreement concerning the establishment of a common European Economic Area (EEA), which should establish between the two regions conditions similar to those of the single market. The negotiations on the EEA have not always proceeded to the satisfaction of both sides. The EC has taken special issue with the inflexible position of the Alpine countries concerning transit. The EFTA countries are, on the other hand, disappointed that they are supposed to accept the single market regulations without receiving a voting privilege. The EC cannot however grant privileges to third parties which not even the European Parliament enjoys.

A voting privilege for the EFTA countries on the decisions of the Community is just as out of the question as a voting privilege for the EC on internal decisions of the EFTA countries. Only EC members can vote. This is now clear to everyone. The EEA negotiations, which in the end were successful, have at least cleared the air and driven out some illusions. The EFTA countries can now decide freely for themselves. The EEA negotiations have already paid off, but hopefully the Community itself has learned something from them. Having presented the alternatives so clearly to the EFTA countries, we must now prepare ourselves for an expansion. The EC will soon be a Community of 18 or even 24 members. There is no way around accepting this as it was clearly shown that membership must be taken seriously and that a partial membership offers no escape from this dilemma.

The Community must therefore prepare itself for a doubling of the membership. That, first of all, presupposes internally-improved decision-making structures. In addition, we must make our desires about further integration objectives more precise. The current status of integration will not significantly influence the new applicants. The EC is developing further and it is important for the candidate countries to know the direction. The members of tomorrow will have a vote even in the next membership discussions. For this reason, the Community must know in advance exactly whom it will allow into these discussions. No new member should be permitted to impede the further integration of Europe. This includes, without question, the readiness to support a common foreign and security policy; 'classical' neutrality makes no sense in a political union which intends to develop into a federated Europe. For this reason, one can caution against the desire to enter the EC solely for economic reasons. In practically all European countries, industry is in favour of joining the EC. But that will hardly be enough to convince the citizens of Austria and Sweden, not to mention those of Norway and Switzerland, that EC membership carries more advantages than disadvantages. Both sides of joining the EC must be argued openly and with controversy if necessary. Otherwise, later irritation is practically preprogrammed.

INTEGRATE THE NEW DEMOCRACIES IN EUROPE

Through overcoming the division of Europe and the downfall of the socialist bloc, the EC suddenly faces new challenges. The principle of the EEC treaty, by which each European democracy can become an EC member if it so desires, is now being truly tested for the first time. The principle was established at a time when Europe was divided into western democracies and eastern dictatorships. Some in the West did not want EC membership at that time; the others in the East could not have it. Through the fall of the iron curtain, the political situation in Europe changed fundamentally. The legacy of socialistic diseconomy in eastern Europe remains strongly divided from that of the West. In order to help eastern Europe to overcome this division, the EC today must offer those countries in middle and eastern Europe a concrete perspective for the future. That includes the offer of full membership.

Of the reform countries, Hungary, the CSFR and Poland have clearly expressed their desire to join. The Baltic states are likewise potential candidates. The opening up of the Community toward the East will make lasting changes in the character of the EC, not only geographically but also politically and institutionally. Geographically, the centre of the Community is shifting toward middle Europe; Berlin will therefore become one of the most significant growth centres in Europe. Politically, countries will be joining the EC which, in light of their past, can be expected to reject emphatically all centralistic tendencies. The EC, which is still in danger of ruling too much and too centrally, can also profit from this. And institutionally, a Community of 18 or 24 members requires completely different decision-making structures in order to remain capable of deciding. Concretely stated, these comprise more majority decisions, more democratic rights for the European Parliament and greater de-centralization. It is not only the countries of middle and eastern Europe which must prepare themselves for membership in the EC; the EC itself must also prepare. It is important here that the efforts occur in parallel, so that the Community's expansion can occur as rapidly as possible.

OPEN UP MARKETS FOR THE REFORM COUNTRIES

In thinking of the future, we cannot forget the present. In the short term, economic stabilization requires the opening of the European single market to these countries. Without access to the market outlets of western Europe, desperately needed direct investment in eastern Europe will largely remain absent. The most valuable thing we can offer the reform countries is to open up the largest market – the market which offers the most purchasing power of any in the world. Initial steps were taken in this direction with the expansion of the preferential customs system, the elimination, or at least setting aside, of quantity-related import restrictions, as well as the increase of the import quotas for textiles from Poland, Hungary, CSFR and the countries formerly belonging to Yugoslavia and the Soviet Union. But truly effective aid represents the complete and final opening of the markets to eastern European products, particularly where our industry will feel the pinch.

There is here and there already understandable resistance to such a market opening toward the East. Potato farmers, textile manufacturers or poultry raisers smell calamity and would like best to see the eastern European producers forced into insignificant corners of the market. But even if market-based structures do not exist everywhere in the East, we must nevertheless open ours, as the Americans did to German or Japanese products after World War II. The argument that we thereby raise our own competition has no merit. Every country is in the long term only as strong as its neighbours. Problems for one quickly become problems for the other. The peoples of Europe live much too closely packed together for any country to be able to view itself as an island of happiness. That will not work, and we therefore must not refuse our solidarity to the middle and eastern European countries.

THE EC BEARS A EUROPE-WIDE RESPONSIBILITY

The EC cannot withdraw from its Europe-wide responsibility. Europe is not helped by well-sounding speeches which cost nothing. If we want to give not only 'stones rather than bread', we have to be ready to take steps which require sacrifices. In a countermove to the opening of the market, the reform countries must create the economic prerequisites for integration, ie, in their own interest accelerate the structural transformation toward a market economy which they are planning anyway. The fact that this is not painless is illustrated by the example of the former German Democratic Republic. But, without a readiness for radical economic reforms in the East, the market opening of the EC would be a one-sided achievement, which would be in danger of remaining ineffective and thereby unpaid for. The reform countries can count on the complete support of the Community, not only in industrial reconstruction but also in expanding their administrative structures. It is in the interest of the West for East and West to move together as closely as possible. There are new perspectives to be derived for EC industry by close cooperation with firms in the reform countries. Just as Japan implemented perfected technology in the countries pressing forward in South-east Asia, so as to be able to optimally use its own capacity and not overheat the labour market, western European industry is presented with a cost-favourable and economically promising interior. If production everywhere in Europe uses uniform technical standards and if labour-intensive manufacturing can be relocated where the labour costs are still relatively low, this also strengthens European industry in worldwide competition with the US and Japan.

The great advantage for Europe is that we Europeans have many neighbours. It is the main concern of European policy that this geographical proximity leads at the same time to neighbourly relations. Industrial cooperation can make a significant contribution to this end.